To Mr. Carnes —

Deo Vindice,

James Edwards

*From the Most Controversial
Talk Show Host in America*

RACISM, SCHMACISM:

*How Liberals Use the "R" Word
to Push the Obama Agenda*

by James Edwards

D0989239

"James Edwards has zeroed in on one of the greatest cultural and social problems of the age, the transformation of self-governing citizens into robots trained to engage in politically correct drivel. The charge of "racism" that resounds everywhere in our society is the most pernicious tool being currently used to create a mood of repression. The author of this book is correct to point out that unless the majority population of this country can be made to throw off the muzzle that they are allowing the thought police to impose on them, there can be no future of freedom for our children or grandchildren."

Paul Gottfried, Ph.D.
Raffensperger Professor of Humanities
Elizabethtown College (PA)
Author; Multiculturalism and the Politics of Guilt:
Toward a Secular Theocracy

"Peter Brimelow once observed that 'the modern definition of a 'racist' is someone who's winning an argument with a liberal.' As James Edwards demonstrates in his enjoyable new book, this definition has recently been expanded to cover 'conservative white person' and even 'white person who meets with other white people in groups.' Linguistically speaking, the word is borderline babble; politically speaking, it's a powerful weapon used to squash dissent and humiliate traditional Americans. Luckily, James is here to show us how to fight back. European Americans — the majority that dares not speak its name — should be proud of their identity and cultural heritage. Being 'racist' means holding views that were once characterized as being 'American.

Richard Spencer
former editor, The American Conservative and Taki's Magazine;
Founder and Executive Editor of AlternativeRight.com.

"James Edwards has shown exceptional courage in creating [and hosting for six years] a trailblazing radio program that provides incisive commentary on the most taboo issues of our day. His determination and his success speak well for the years of home schooling that punctuated his education.

"From the perspective of Emeritus Professor at Vanderbilt University School of Medicine, I have the luxury of being retired and therefore with relatively little to lose from speaking out. Not so with James. He is beginning. He has a young family. He is taking risks now, with his career and in the court of public opinion, so that his growing family can look forward to living in a free and prosperous country.

"I look foward to the publication of James' first book, which is sure to be full of facts and ideas that are both provocative and innovative."

Virginia Deane Abernethy, Ph.D.
Professor Emeritus of Psychiatry [Anthropology]
Vanderbilt University School of Medicine
Nashville, TN

Racism, Schmacism:
How Liberals Use the "R" Word
to Push the Obama Agenda

by James Edwards

ISBN-10: 1-452-85613-3
ISBN-13/EAN-13: 978-1-452-85613-1

Published in the United States of America
by TPC Press

Book Design by Creative Business Graphics

This book is dedicated to my two families.

First and foremost, to my personal family. To my wife, for her unwavering support and devotion throughout a wonderfully turbulent political career. To my parents, for raising me as a good and decent Southern gentleman. To my grandparents, who showed me unconditional love. To my brother and cousins, who are always there for me. And to my friends, for all the good times we've shared.

Secondly, this book is dedicated to my political family. To the staff and crew of The Political Cesspool Radio Program, both past and present, who have built with me a remarkable monument of grassroots activism that continues to stand the test of time. To the guests of the show who have given their talents to give us substance. Last but never least, to the fans of TPC, whose support sustains me when our enemies attack.

I love you all.

TABLE OF CONTENTS

CHAPTER 1

Welcome to Post-Racial Paradise, Blue-Eyed Devils!

So, conservatives, how's that whole post-racial America thing workin' out for ya?

Yeah, me neither!

Remember the New America the media promised us back in the run-up to the 2008 election? You know, the one Barack Obama was going to usher in when he became America's first black president? It was supposed to be a glorious new day that was dawning in the good old U.S. of A. Obama was going to be the leader we've all supposedly been longing for, the one who would break down the barriers of race that have kept us divided for so long. He was the ideal man for the job, we were told, because he had a white mother and a black father. He would be a bridge between two separate and unequal worlds, and his background would enable him to bring us together as one people, finally ushering in true equality between the races, and uniting us into a stronger nation than we've ever been.

Barack Obama, the media assured us time and time again, was nothing compared to Jesse Jackson or Al Sharpton, whose inflammatory rhetoric and well-known personal problems had unfortunately prevented them from bringing blacks and whites together. (It's kind of weird though that until quite recently the media has always presented Jackson and Sharpton as authentic black leaders, and blamed their unpopularity among white people on racism.) Obama was a new kind of black leader, and white people had nothing to fear from him. Sure, he was going to look out for the interests of black folks, but he was going to be just as vigilant to make sure whites were treated fairly. After all, his mother was white! Obama was going to be sort of a civil rights activist for everybody.

Of course, there were a few bumps along the way.

Certain people began circulating a video of one of Obama's public appearances where he didn't put his hand over his heart during the national anthem. Others noticed that he had quit wearing his American flag lapel pin. But no worries; Obama assured us that he just doesn't like wearing his patriotism on his sleeve. He prefers the true, inner patriotism to the cheap, phony public displays of it. And only a racist would be upset over these things.

Then, some people tried to make a big deal out of his association with William Ayers, a former terrorist with the Weather Underground in the 1960s. Ayers in 2001 had been photographed standing on an American flag, and was quoted as saying that the terrorists of the 1960s hadn't done enough."[1] That Obama would be friends with a man like that seemed to be cause for alarm, but both he and the media assured us that they were merely slight acquaintances who happened to live in the same neighborhood. And, oh yeah, anyone who said differently was a racist.

Then there was a bit of unpleasantness over Reverend Jeremiah Wright and Trinity United Church of Christ. Video clips of some of Rev. Wright's sermons began appearing on the Internet, and then on national television, where he was shouting, "God Damn America!" and referring to this nation as "the U.S.

---

[1] http://www.chicagomag.com/Chicago-Magazine/August-2001/No-Regrets

of KKK A." A lot of Americans were naturally confused and upset. This was the church that Obama has been attending for nearly twenty years? This was the man Obama considered his mentor, and respected so much that he borrowed one of his sermon titles for his best selling book? You no doubt remember the uproar that briefly ensued. But then Obama gave a real pretty speech in Philadelphia, and the media told us the case was closed. Anyone who would dare bring up Obama's church or pastor after that speech was nothing but a stone cold racist.

And millions of white Americans ate it up. Looking at the big picture, these things were no big deal. Can Obama help it if one of his neighbors happens to be a former terrorist? Heck no! And sure, maybe Jeremiah Wright said some crazy things, but we all know that black churches aren't quite as uptight as white worship services, and it's to be expected that a black preacher would sometimes go too far. It's hardly anything to get excited about. He just has a different way of showing how much he loves Jesus, that's all.

Heck, even the GOP candidate for president, John McCain, said he wasn't going to make an issue of Obama's nearly 20-year membership in Trinity United Church of Christ. The fact that Obama not only sat in the pews of that church listening to Jeremiah Wright for most of his adult life, but also gave the church tens of thousands of dollars, and named his book after one of Wright's sermons, had absolutely nothing to do with anything at all. Anyone who felt otherwise was not welcome in his campaign.

McCain actually repudiated a North Carolina GOP ad for mentioning Jeremiah Wright![1] He also denounced Bill Cunningham, a conservative talk show host who emceed one of his campaign appearances. What horrible sin did Bill Cunningham commit? He had the nerve to refer to McCain's opponent by his name, Barack Hussein Obama.[2] McCain was so afraid of being seen as a racist it's a wonder he didn't drop out of the race and endorse Obama. I don't know how he was

[2]http://thecaucus.blogs.nytimes.com/2008/02/26/mccain-repudiates-hussein-obama-remarks/

able to sleep at night knowing he might be standing in the way of America's first black president.

Well, John McCain must be sleeping like a baby these days, because his 100-Percent-Grade-A-Certified Racism-Free campaign was no threat to the Obama team. As Rush Limbaugh put it after the liberal media heaped praise on him for his "gracious" concession speech, "McCain's entire campaign was a concession speech." Obama mopped the floor with him. McCain could have won the White House if he hadn't been so afraid of being called racist. Just imagine how different the election would have turned out had McCain been running TV ads focusing on Obama's love of Jeremiah Wright and his shockingly frank hatred of white people. The McCain campaign staff actually filmed a very effective ad about Jeremiah Wright, but McCain refused to run it, because he didn't want to be called a racist. So he refused to speak about what would have been a winning issue, and he lost. Badly.

And he got called racist anyway. So that worked out real well.

See, John McCain apparently hasn't figured out this whole "racism" game yet. Tens of millions of other white people don't seem to get it, either. A lot of white folks voted for Obama because they thought it would be racist not to. As soon as the new president started filling his cabinet, they found out that they, too, were racists. Not just racists, but cowards. Attorney General Eric Holder informed us that we are a nation of cowards and racists, and that deep down, things haven't changed all that much since the 1950s when it comes to race. Being called racists and cowards was the thanks white people got for voting for Obama.

A few months later, the Tea Party phenomenon began, capturing the attention of both the news media and pundits. Thousands of people came out in cities all across America to oppose the big spending proposals by the White House and the Democrat-controlled Congress. And what was the reaction of most of the media? Was it to seek to understand and explain the growing anger and frustration on the part of millions of voters at what's going on in Washington, DC?

Ha! Yeah, that's a good one!

No, they just called the protesters racists who had no legitimate concerns, but were simply using their alleged grievances to cover up the fact that they hated Obama because he's black. A few months later, when thousands more came out to Town Hall meetings to protest Obama's radical plans for America's health care system, it was the same reaction. Those protesters weren't really opposed to socialized medicine in America; they just hate the idea of a black president, and are simply inventing excuses to denounce him.

Many white people, both liberal and conservative, are shocked at this turn of events. They were certain that with a black man in the White House, charges of racism and hate would begin dying down, and that race would become a smaller and smaller factor in American life from here on out. Whether they voted for Obama or McCain, none of them would have believed last November that America's first black Attorney General, appointed by America's first black president, would have the unbelievable gall to lecture them on racism.

Well, they shouldn't have been shocked. I could have told them that not only would electing a black president do nothing to reduce charges of racism, but would only make things worse. A lot worse. And there is no end in sight. Because to the media and the Democrats and the "civil rights" groups, the word "racist" doesn't mean what people like you and your neighbor think it means. That's why people are so shocked when they're labeled racist in the media for disagreeing with Obama. They're horrified at the idea of being a racist, and can't fathom where the liberals get off accusing them of being one.

Well, after you've read this book, you'll understand exactly what liberals mean by the terms "racism" and "racist," and you won't be intimidated by these phony charges and accusations anymore.

You'll finally understand what they're trying to do by throwing these labels around.

You'll also learn just how high the stakes are, and why conservatives keep losing the cultural and political battles.

You'll learn the one thing the liberals and the media elites fear most, and how calling us "racist" keeps us from utilizing the one weapon that can defeat them.

And, finally, you'll understand how to fight back, and how to start winning.

CHAPTER 2

John McCain Isn't a Racist, But He's Still a Racist

You know what the funniest thing is when it comes to all this controversy about criticism of President Obama being racist? It's the fact that John McCain could have easily won the 2008 election for the White House. Obviously, if McCain had won, we wouldn't even be having this discussion. We could oppose all these huge bailouts and government takeovers, or Cabinet appointments or military policies and the media wouldn't be calling us a bunch of racists every time we raised an objection. Of course, they'd still be calling us reactionaries, stingy, paranoid, and lots of other names, but they've been doing that for decades to conservatives. And they would, without a doubt, be declaring that the only reason Obama didn't win was racism. But at least we wouldn't be getting called racists simply for disagreeing with the president.

So next time you see a media figure, Hollywood celebretard, Democrat politician, or some other bleeding heart liberal call a conservative a racist for disagreeing with Obama, be sure to send John McCain a postcard and say "Hey, thanks John! We really appreciate it!" Because if John McCain had waged a real campaign, one where he really took the fight to Barack Hussein Obama, it's very likely he would have won. He didn't do that at all; in fact, he pretty much did the exact opposite. He rolled over and played dead for Obama, and allowed Obama to walk all over him. Why? For one reason: he didn't want to be called a racist. So he pulled his punches, and refused to go after Obama where he was most vulnerable, on the one issue that really could have connected with average Americans when it came to why they should vote for him and not Obama, which was Obama's long membership in Trinity United Church of Christ, and his love for "Rev." Jeremiah Wright, a man who clearly hates white people.

And if you think that there was more to it than that, and that there has to be another explanation for McCain running such a weak and pathetic campaign, then you'll have to come up with a real good reason for his embarrassingly anemic performance. Because McCain has never been known for being afraid to mix it up when running for office, and he's been in politics for a long time. In fact, he himself has openly bragged about just how down and dirty he's willing to get during campaign time.

There is a widely reported quote attributed to John McCain when he appeared before a group of people from the National Republican Senatorial Committee, where he explained that he was willing to do whatever it took to win his Senate race: "I play to win. I do whatever it takes to win. If I have to f*** my opponent to win, I'll do it. If I have to destroy my opponent, I won't give it a second thought."[3]

That's pretty cut and dried. He's making no bones about it: when it comes to running for office, John McCain is going to play hardball. But that wasn't the John McCain we saw in 2008, not by a long shot. Some might object to the fact that this particular quote was from back in the 1980s when he was first running for Senate, and McCain has mellowed out quite a bit since then. Really? Then what about the 2000 presidential primaries,

---

[3]http://www.capitolhillblue.com/node/10086?page=2

when he was in a tight race with George W. Bush for the GOP nomination?

McCain had absolutely no qualms about attacking Bush for the endorsements he received from Jerry Falwell and Pat Robertson, and he denounced the two evangelical leaders as "agents of intolerance"[4] with "an evil influence"[5] over the Republican Party. Sorry, but the "older, mellower John McCain" argument doesn't hold much water.

No, McCain's weakness was all about one thing: race. He was running against a black man, and evidently the thought of being the candidate who kept Barack Hussein Obama from becoming America's first black president was too much of a strain on his conscience. McCain loves to say that voting against making Martin Luther King, Jr.'s birthday a national holiday was the "worst mistake" he ever made as a Senator, and that he's had to deal with the burden of guilt he bears because of that vote for years. Well, if voting against honoring Martin Luther King, Jr. with a national holiday is still eating at McCain's tender conscience after a quarter-century, you can only imagine how he would have felt had he beaten Obama. Heck, he probably would have been downright suicidal! So he basically threw the election, and the campaign was over before it began. His race for the White House was over from the start when he made it clear that he was not going to make Jeremiah Wright an issue in the 2008 campaign. He was "taking the high road," and "refusing to engage in the politics of destruction." Blah, blah, blah.

Yeah, right!

No, McCain didn't run an ineffective, losing campaign because of his tender conscience, or his newly discovered dislike of negative politics. He did it because he was scared to death of being called a racist, and he knew that if he treated Obama like he would've treated a white candidate, the media would've torn him a new one, and he would've been doing nothing but dodging accusations of racism for the entire campaign. John McCain

---

[4]http://tech.mit.edu/V120/N9/mccain_right_9.9w.html
[5]http://www.nytimes.com/2008/05/24/opinion/24sat2.html

has always been a darling of the press, the media's favorite Republican (because he's such a "maverick," don't ya know), and he wanted to stay on their good side.

In 2000, he knew he would win points with the media by denouncing Jerry Falwell and Pat Robertson, because they were white conservatives, and the media hates them. But if he had attacked Barack Obama's hate-filled lunatic preacher or, God forbid, Obama himself for staying in Wright's church for nearly twenty years and giving him tens of thousands of dollars, that would have been a whole different story. Why? Because Wright and Obama are black. Never mind that the "intolerance" preached by Jerry Falwell and Pat Robertson back then doesn't even come close to the kind of hate Jeremiah Wright was preaching. Falwell and Robertson were white, so it was fine to slander them in 2000. But Jeremiah Wright is black, so it's unspeakably evil to tell the truth about him.

John McCain lost, and he lost badly, because he decided it was better to lose the election than to be called a racist, no matter how unfounded the charges. So he went around denouncing people associated with his campaign who dared refer to Barack Hussein Obama by his legal name, and he repudiated an ad run by a state GOP group that featured Jeremiah Wright screaming "God damn America!" And what good did it do him? Not a bit. All the cowardice he displayed in a desperate attempt to avoid being called the "R-word" was for nothing. Obama himself accused McCain of running a racist campaign on at least two occasions. He told a crowd at a June fundraiser: "We know what kind of campaign they're going to run. They're going to try to make you afraid. They're going to try to make you afraid of me. He's young and inexperienced and he's got a funny name. And did I mention he's black?"[6] A month later, Obama played the racism card again, accusing McCain of trying to scare people out of voting for Obama because "he doesn't look like all those other presidents on the dollar bills."[7]

---

[6]http://www.reuters.com/article/politicsNews/idUSN2040982720080620
[7]http://abcnews.go.com/GMA/Politics/story?id=5495348&page=1&page=1

You would think that McCain would get the message after those two incidents. That he would have taken the advice of Internet pundit Steve Sailer: he could either do what it takes to win by getting tough on Obama and Wright and being called a racist, or he could forfeit the election by refusing to mount a serious challenge to Obama because he's black, and lose — "and still get smeared as a racist by the media."[8] But no, McCain didn't listen to Steve Sailer, and the attacks just kept coming. When he released a lighthearted ad poking fun at Obama's inexperience and the media's adoration of him by comparing Obama to Paris Hilton and Britney Spears, the media kicked it into high gear. This was no good-natured poke at Obama's celebrity treatment by the press; no, it was nothing less than the most ugly kind of "racist imagery" imaginable. What McCain was actually doing, according to the media, was not-so-subtly playing to white people's "hang-ups" about sex between black men and white women. I kid you not.

Bob Herbert of the New York Times called the ad "foul" and "poisonous" and said it was "designed to exploit the hostility, anxiety and resentment of the many white Americans who are still freakishly hung up on the idea of black men rising above their station and becoming sexually involved with white women."[9] (Herbert also claimed that the ad featured the Leaning Tower of Pisa and the Washington Monument, and that the McCain people had put them in there as "phallic symbols."[10] Herbert's eyesight is as bad as his judgment, as neither tower appears in the ad. You could make a good case that Bob Herbert is freakishly hung up on interracial sex, slander and phallic symbols. But you'd better not — Bob Herbert is black, so that would be racist. His column displayed keen insights and dazzling brilliance, and don't you forget it!)

It wasn't just Bob Herbert. Many, many people in the media parroted the same line, as anyone can verify with a quick

[8]http://www.vdare.com/sailer/081109_gop.htm
[9]http://www.nytimes.com/2008/08/02/opinion/02herbert.html?_r=2?ef=slogin
[10]http://newsbusters.org/blogs/mark-finkelstein/2008/08/04/obamania-has-herbert-hallucinating

Internet search. Here's Bill Press, Pat Buchanan's old foil on Crossfire:

> "In juxtaposing Barack Obama with Britney Spears and Paris Hilton, the McCain campaign is simply trying to plant the old racist seed of a black man hitting on young white woman. Not directly, but subliminally and disgracefully. One thing for sure: this isn't the John McCain we first saw in 2000, running a campaign on the issues. And this isn't the positive McCain campaign he himself promised us for 2008. This is a campaign that, from the beginning, is nothing but negative, personal, dirty and, yes, racist."[11]

Now if that episode didn't make McCain realize that all his pussyfooting around wasn't going to do him a darned bit of good, and he was going to be called a vile racist no matter what he did, so he might as well take the gloves off, then nothing was going to get it across to him. He was bound and determined to play by the media rules that a white candidate playing hardball against a black candidate, treating him just as he'd treat a white guy running against him, is flat out racism. By God, he might lose, and he might get called racist, but he'd get called racist a lot more if he did what it took to win, and there was no way he was going to let that happen.

And thanks to John McCain's fear of being called a racist, Barack Obama is in the White House, and now anyone who disagrees with him is a racist.

Be sure and send McCain that thank you note!

---

[11]http://www.huffingtonpost.com/bill-press/john-mccain-plays-the-rac_b_116042.html

CHAPTER 3

Anti-Klan Books Are Racist!

Let's meet another horrible racist.

As we've seen, these evil racists are everywhere in America — under every rock, behind every bush, and in every nook and cranny. No place, no matter how big it is, or how respected it is, is immune from racism. So it should come as no surprise that this shocking case of hideous racism took place at one of America's biggest and best-known public university systems, Indiana University. That's right; racists are running amok in America's heartland! If you don't believe me, just read on.

Keith John Sampson is a man in his early 50s who, in 2007, was a student at Indiana University-Purdue University Indianapolis (IUPUI). He was also working as a janitor at the university. If you look him up on the Internet, you'll see that Keith John Sampson looks innocent enough, seemingly just another mild mannered, middle-aged man. Anyone looking at his picture would see nothing out of the ordinary, and would hardly think there was any cause for concern. But don't be fooled by appearances, because his innocent look is nothing but a front. Behind that mask is one of the most vicious and despicable racists in the United States. In fact, Keith Sampson is so filled with vile racism that he couldn't keep it to himself, but had to shove his hate down the throats of his black co-workers in the janitorial department at IUPUI.

They put up with Keith Sampson's racism for a while, but eventually it became too much to bear, and one of his black co-workers finally complained about the horrible situation. To their credit, once the higher ups at IUPUI learned about this intolerable situation, they took swift, decisive action. The Office of Affirmative Action at IUPUI notified Sampson that he was obviously and unquestionably guilty of racial harassment, and that if he didn't knock it off at once, he'd be risking his job.

So exactly how was Keith John Sampson committing "racial harassment" against his black co-workers? He was reading a book during his break periods.

A book?

Yes, a book. Don't think reading a book can't be racist. Racism comes in all kinds of shapes and forms.

Gosh, what kind of horrible book was Keith John Sampson reading in front of his black co-workers, anyway? *Mein Kampf? I Hate Black People? Death to Colored Folks?*

Oh, no... the book he was reading was much more insidious than that. It was called *Notre Dame vs. The Klan: How the Fighting Irish Defeated the Ku Klux Klan*. It's the story of how, back in the 1920s, the KKK (who were anti-Catholic) decided to go to South Bend, Indiana and harass the students at the University of Notre Dame. The Notre Dame community decided to fight back, and their organized opposition to the KKK drove the Klan out of town in an embarrassing defeat.

Now at this point you're probably scratching your head and wondering just what exactly is "racist" about reading a book that celebrates a bunch of college kids defeating the Ku Klux Klan.

Do you know why you're having trouble understanding this episode?

It's because you're a racist, too!

Because only a racist would have any problem seeing just how racist it is to read a book like this in front of black people. It doesn't matter if the book is denouncing the KKK or not. The only thing that matters is that a black person saw the words "Klan" and "KKK" on the book cover, and decided it was a racist book, and Keith Sampson was a racist for reading it.

As the head of IUPUI's Office of Affirmative Action explained it to Sampson in an official letter of reprimand, all "reasonable" people would know without being told that reading a book denouncing the KKK in front of black people is racist:

"Upon review of this matter, we conclude that your conduct constitutes racial harassment in that you demonstrated disdain and insensitivity to your co-workers who repeatedly requested that you refrain from reading the book which has such an inflammatory and offensive topic in their presence. You contend that you weren't aware of the offensive nature of the topic and were reading the book about the KKK to better understand discrimination. However you used extremely poor judgment by insisting on openly reading the book related to a historically and racially abhorrent subject in the presence of your Black co-workers. Furthermore, employing the legal 'reasonable person standard,' a majority of adults are aware of and understand how repugnant the KKK is to African-Americans, their reactions to the Klan, and the reasonableness of the request that you not read the book in their presence.

"During your meeting with Marguerite Watkins, Assistant Affirmative Action Officer [sic] you were instructed to stop reading the book in the immediate presence of your co-workers and when reading the book to sit apart from the immediate proximity of these co-workers. Please be advised, any future substantiated conduct of a similar nature could result in serious disciplinary action."[12]

Well, there ya go. That letter was written by Lillian Charleston, the black woman who has been the Affirmative Action Officer at IUPUI for over fifteen years, and gets paid over $100,000 a year to spot racism.[13]

So I think she knows what she's talking about.

Now, don't you feel silly for wondering how reading an anti-racism book could be called racist?

---

[12]http://www.takimag.com/sniperstower/article/how_dare_you_read_that_in_front_of_me/
[13]http://www.newswithviews.com/Duke/selwyn92.htm

CHAPTER 4

Nation of Cowards

Boy, did white Americans get a surprise in late February 2009 from their new president! There they were, basking in the glow of self-congratulation for electing America's first black head of state. The honeymoon had just begun; for many liberal whites, it was a euphoric time. Obama's victory was like the moon landing, the discovery of the polio vaccine, and winning the lottery all rolled into one, and they were still swooning over just how fantastic it is that America has gotten past race, and now we can say for the first time in our history that truly anyone can grow up to be president.

But the euphoria didn't last long. The honeymoon was pretty much over after newly confirmed Attorney General Eric Holder gave a big speech and said that when it comes to race, we're a nation of cowards, and that when you get right down to it, race relations haven't improved much in 50 years. That was certainly a fine how-do-ya-do! Being called cowards was *not* what the white folks who voted for Obama wanted to hear.

Not by a long shot. The media, of course, played the speech up for all it was worth and naturally the media elites pretty much all agreed with Holder and praised him for his "courage" in making such a "gutsy" speech.

Oh yeah, it took real "courage" to say the same thing that the media has been preaching for the last several decades, along with the NAACP, the Democratic Party, and nearly every public school teacher and college professor in America. Holder was really going out on a limb by agreeing with the liberal power structure. I don't know where he found the guts to take such a bold, lonely stand.

But I'm certainly glad he did find the "courage" to give his now-famous speech. Because it woke up a lot of white liberals and "moderates." Not only were they shocked to hear Holder condemn them for their "cowardice," they were also outraged. How dare anyone call them a coward after they had done The Right Thing, and voted for the black guy? Talk about harshing a buzz! Where does this guy get off calling them cowards?! To paraphrase Michelle Obama, for the first time in my adult life I actually felt sorry for liberals. Holder's speech was a classic example of biting the hand that feeds you. Without the support of white moderates and liberals, who desperately wanted to vote for a black man for president, Obama didn't stand a chance of being in the White House. He never would have gotten past Hillary in the primaries. If he had somehow survived the primaries, McCain would have mopped the floor with him if it weren't for the millions of white people who pulled the Democrat lever because they wanted to "get past race" in America.

And how does he thank them? He sends Eric Holder out to attack them as cowards, and to say that they're not much better than Bull Connor and the night riders of the early 1960s. Oh sure, Holder said, you like to think you're progressive because you work with some black folks but, when the work day is over, you head for your white families and your white neighborhoods and stay there. Then on the weekends you watch your sports with your white buddies, go shopping with your fellow white soccer moms, and go to your white churches. Holder really stressed the point about churches, regurgitating Martin Luther King, Jr.'s old line about 11 o'clock on Sunday morning being the most segregated hour in America. Hang on to that thought, because I want to come back to it.

First, though, I want to make a point that I don't remember very many people raising after Eric Holder made his "courageous" speech. A lot of conservatives disagreed with him by quibbling over the details. They talked about how their family had adopted a black kid from Haiti. Or they said that Holder didn't know what he was talking about because they had blacks and Hispanics at the Super Bowl party they threw at their house. And many of them went on and on about just how integrated their churches are.

Their point was that Eric Holder had no idea what he was talking about, and that they don't need lectures on "racism" from someone who's so clueless that he thinks race relations haven't improved in the last fifty years.

Sorry, folks, but that was the wrong answer. They walked right into Eric Holder's (and Obama's) trap, by letting Holder set the rules of the "conversation on race" he supposedly wants Americans to start having. And as long as we keep letting these people set the rules when it comes to "racism," we can never win. It's a rigged game, and all of our protesting that *we most certainly aren't racist* won't mean a thing.

So how should conservatives have responded? It's very simple. We should have told Eric Holder and Barack Obama that where we live, who we're friends with, and where we go to church is *none of their damn business*! Evidently, liberty and freedom are alien concepts to people like Holder and Obama. They think they have the right to tell us who to associate with, how to worship God, in addition to thinking they have the authority to condemn us as cowards and racists, *and* hector us if we're not associating with the right people, or going to the correct church.

We shouldn't be surprised at this attitude coming from these jokers. The "civil rights" bunch has always believed they have the right to tell us who we can and can't associate with, and now they're running the country. No, that's hardly unexpected. The real shocker in this whole affair is how conservatives willingly accepted the idea that Washington, D.C. has every right to tell us how to live our private lives. Instead of telling Eric Holder and Barack Obama where to get off, that this is a free country and we'll be friends with whomever we want and go to church wherever we darn well please—and if they don't like it they can go to hell—we turned into a bunch of wimps and agreed to play their game, by their rules. We fully accepted their premise that it's their job to tell us how to live; we just protested that they weren't giving us enough credit for being good little non-racist boys and girls.

And we wonder why we can never win when it comes to "racism?"

As you can see, I was pretty angry about this episode. And I'm still angry. I could write a whole book about nothing but Eric Holder's speech and how conservatives reacted to it. In fact, there are so many things wrong with this situation that I don't even know where to begin, but I've got to start somewhere. The one thing that people probably found most galling was the absurdity of the situation. No doubt about it, it took a lot of gall to make that speech. Here was America's first black Attorney General, appointed by America's first black president, and his first major speech is all about what a horribly racist country America is! I'm surprised we didn't hear the theme from *The Twilight Zone* playing in the background or that at the end of the speech, Ashton Kutcher didn't come out and announce America had just been punk'd!

Secondly, let's go back to the church thing, because that really took a lot of gall. Not to put too fine a point on it, but when is the last time that the federal government showed any respect whatsoever for Christianity? The last fifty years have been marked by one assault after another from Washington, D.C. on our nation's Christian heritage. Bible reading was tossed out of schools. Prayer was banned in schools. Passing out New Testaments in schools was ruled a violation of the Constitution. Nativity scenes at the local courthouse have been outlawed. The list goes on and on, and it hasn't stopped. Pro-lifers and anti-immigration activists were recently labeled "potential terrorists" who need to be watched by the Department of Homeland Security. Even a Republican like George W. Bush refused to call a Christmas tree a Christmas tree, instead referring to it as a "holiday tree." And now, D.C. wants to lecture us that we're not practicing Christianity the right way? Gimme a break.

You'd think that the Attorney General of the United States would be familiar with the First Amendment to the Constitution, which explicitly prohibits the federal government from meddling in religious affairs. It's no accident that freedom to practice religion without government interference is the first right mentioned in the very first plank of the Bill of Rights. The founding fathers thought freedom of religion was so important that they listed it before all other rights, such as free speech and a free press. So where does the nation's top law enforcement official get off telling us with whom we should and shouldn't go to church? Eric Holder's speech was nothing less than a frontal assault on the First Amendment to the Constitution. He was serving notice that from now on, it will be the government's business to meddle in your religious practices, if they don't believe that your church is sufficiently non-white. That's exactly what Eric Holder's speech was aimed at — using his position as Attorney General to tell you where you can or can't go to church. His opinion may not yet have the force of law, but that's just a matter of time unless we stand up for our rights before it's too late.

As the recent history of America makes clear, liberals like nothing better than imposing their morality on others. They've never had "a good idea" they didn't want to force down other people's throats. Why should we expect it will be any different with this notion coming out of Washington D.C. that some churches are "good" because they're racially mixed, while other ones are "bad" because they're too white? They did it with our schools, even though the Constitution gives the feds absolutely no authority over local schools. And you really think they won't try it with our churches? Don't be surprised if, in a few years, the government starts talking about repealing the tax exemption of "racist" churches. And they won't mean churches like the one Obama used to go to, where blackness was at the center of their theology and church services. No, that's fine, because they're black. When Eric Holder and Obama talk about "racist" churches, they're talking about churches with "too many" white people. And, obviously, they think "something must be done" about these horrible, racist bastions of segregation. Today, it's the top law enforcement official in America condemning "racist" churches; in a few years it will be D.C. passing laws and making court decisions to deal with "the problem."

Of course, many people will object that that's preposterous. "That's crazy talk, James. They could never do that. It would violate the Constitution!" Well, since when has anyone in Washington, D.C. cared about the Constitution? Was there ever a crazier scheme than school busing? Where does the Constitution provide for the federal government to force local schools to bus kids all over town to come up with the "right" racial mix? Nowhere. There is nothing like that in the Constitution, not even remotely, yet it didn't stop liberal courts from imposing that insanity on America. Besides, if you've been paying attention the last few decades, you're no doubt well aware that the current view of the founding fathers among liberals and the media is that they don't deserve any respect, because they were a bunch of racists who killed the Indians, enslaved blacks, only allowed white males to vote, and only wanted white people to immigrate here.

Because of this racism, the Constitution is horribly tainted, and one of these days will have to be rewritten for a multiracial America. (Yes, there are actually people who believe this — many of them are teaching at colleges and high schools.) Until that day comes, however, the federal government is free to ignore the Constitution in order to advance "diversity" and "fight racism." Don't think they won't do it. Eric Holder's "nation of cowards" speech was designed to help bring that day about, by getting people used to the idea that it's the federal government's business to decide which churches are "racist" and which ones aren't. Judging by the lack of outrage from mainstream conservatives, it looks like his speech did exactly that.

CHAPTER 5

Poking Fun at Obama is Racism

Did you hear about the "absolute hate crime" committed against Barack Obama?

Gosh, that sounds awful. An absolute hate crime? What happened? Did a neo-Nazi beat him up at an appearance? Did somebody burn a cross on the White House lawn?

Uh, no. Someone made fun of Obama.

Yes, that's all there is to it.

No, I'm not kidding. It happened in August 2008, when Obama was in the thick of his campaign for the White House. The site of this "absolute hate crime" was the Evergreen State Fair in Monroe, Washington. Here are the shocking details: Someone was selling $3 bills making fun of Obama. The obviously phony "currency" featured a cartoon of Obama in Arab headgear, with signatures from "spiritual advisor" Al Sharpton, and a caption under Obama saying "Da Man."[14]

Gosh, isn't that terrible? Showing Obama in Arab headgear.

---

[14]http://seattletimes.nwsource.com/html/localnews/2008140846_fair27m0.html

How much worse can it get? Apparently, not very much. One woman quoted by the Seattle paper that reported the story, described the humorous currency as "an absolute hate crime," I kid you not. She was a volunteer at the Democratic Party booth at the fair. You expect that sort of response from a Democrat — that's why they're Democrats. Unfortunately, just as we saw with John McCain, the local Republican leadership was completely spineless in this incident. The Republican County chairwoman denounced the bills, calling them "offensive," ordered them removed and not brought back, and then apologized. Gosh, I wonder why the GOP just can't seem to win elections anymore?

If this had been an isolated incident, it would've been bad enough. Unfortunately, it was just one example of many. In "post-racial" America, making fun of Obama, or any other black politician, or any non-white person for that matter, is racist.

For years I've been saying that diversity and free speech can't long coexist. And every year more and more speech is condemned by groups like the Anti-Defamation League (ADL), the Southern Policy Law Center (SPLC), and the NAACP as "hate speech." And an ever-increasing number of articles in law reviews and academic journals make the argument that the First Amendment doesn't protect "hate speech." That message is slowly but surely working its way into the public mind. Any time someone passes out politically incorrect flyers in a neighborhood — no matter how innocuous they are — the local police precinct is flooded with calls from concerned citizens reporting "the crime." Now that we have a black president, any ridicule of or disagreement with him is "racist hate speech" and must not be allowed.

Ridiculing presidential candidates has a long and rich history in America, going all the way back to its beginning, and no one ever tried to seriously claim that making fun of the candidate you don't like should be illegal. But those days are gone. Oh, sure, you can still make fun of white candidates all you want. Heck, you still hear Dan Quayle jokes on late night TV, nearly twenty years after he left office. But making fun of a black guy is way out of line. If you doubt it, just look at what happened back in 2008, when Barack Obama was running for president. As we've already seen, John McCain denounced his own supporters for just calling Barack Obama by his legal name. (I know...hard to believe McCain lost, huh?)

That was just the tip of the iceberg, however. Earlier in 2008, the mainstream media went into hysterics because a man in Marietta, Georgia had a few hundred t-shirts printed up that said "Obama 2008," right next to a picture of the famous cartoon monkey named Curious George. If you're under the age of 60, you're no doubt familiar with Curious George, the lovable little monkey that goes on all kinds of adventures in children's books. He's famous the world over, and very popular. He also doesn't look a thing like an actual monkey, as everyone who has ever seen the books knows. He's actually made to appear quite human in his facial features. The bar owner said he'd gotten the idea because Obama sort of looks like Curious George.

The left-wing liberals in politics and the media knew better, however. It seems that liberals, whenever they see or hear anything about monkeys, apes, or chimps, automatically think about black people. So then they turn around and accuse everyone else who ever mentions monkeys, apes or chimps in any context remotely related to a black person of being a "racist." Psychologists call it "projection;" it refers to the habit of accusing others of what you're guilty of yourself. Liberals do it all the time; this is just one of the more blatant examples. White liberal guilt is a heavy burden to bear. It makes people say and do very strange things.

Seeing "racism" in the Obama comparison to Curious George is very strange, indeed. Curious George is a world famous cartoon character known to people all across the planet, and universally loved. His character is smart and inquisitive, happy and fun loving, which are hardly negative traits to ascribe to anyone. As I pointed out, he also isn't really a monkey; his face looks far more like a human's than it does a monkey's. After all, it's a cartoon, for crying out loud. Plus, with his beige face and prominent ears, it's hardly surprising that someone would see a resemblance to Barack Obama. (There. I said it! Please don't sue me!) Making a funny observation about a president's resemblance to a popular children's cartoon character would be cute if McCain were president, but he's white. Obama is black, though, so it's "racism."

So the liberal media's "outrage" over a couple hundred Curious George/Obama t-shirts that no one would have ever heard of if it weren't for the very same liberal media turning it into a national news story is crazy. But it's not only crazy; it's also proof of their incredible hypocrisy when it comes to race and "racism" in America. *Because Barack Obama isn't the first president to be compared to a monkey.* He is also not the first one to be compared to the Curious George cartoon character. In fact, liberals spent the eight years prior to Obama's administration doing the very same things to George Bush, but on a much bigger scale. Countless websites had pictures of Bush next to a chimp with the same facial expression. Countless others used computer technology to morph his face into that of a monkey's. And, obviously, with a first name like George, it goes without saying that many of them referred to President Bush as Curious George, in both words and artwork.

You don't have to take my word for this. The proof is all over the Internet. Just go to your favorite search engine and run a search on "george bush monkey," "george bush chimp," "george bush curious george," etc. Be sure to check the image results, too. You'll see for yourself that this stuff was everywhere on liberal websites for eight years, many of them very prominent ones that get a ton of traffic. One popular site which was devoted to ridiculing George Bush by comparing him to a primate was even called www.smirkingchimp.com.

Yet do you recall the mainstream media ever raising a peep about any of this? Did they ever point to these websites and denounce them? Did they ever say that no one should compare President Bush to a chimp or a monkey, that that sort of thing was outside the bounds of decent political commentary? I certainly don't remember hearing or reading anything like that from the mainstream media, even as millions of people logged on to these mocking websites over the years. But let the owner of a tiny bar in a small town print up a few t-shirts comparing a black presidential candidate to a lovable cartoon monkey who looks like a human, and it's suddenly horrible "racism," and national news? Why is it fine to compare a white president to a monkey, and do it in a vicious manner, but it's wrong to humorously compare a black presidential candidate to one?

Liberals will tell you that it's because, in America's past, some white people mocked blacks by saying they were related to primates. OK, now I'm really confused...according to the mainstream media, aren't we all supposed to be related to primates? Isn't that what they are constantly telling us? In addition, don't they mock conservative Christians for believing that God, not evolution, created humans? So exactly what's the problem? Does that make any sense to you? Yeah, me neither. And once you realize what the media is up to with all this "racism" business, you'll understand that they're just making the rules up as they go along, and the rules about "racism" have only one goal — to shut white people up. That's why the rules are so contradictory — the very same behavior or speech from a white person, denounced and condemned 24/7 on the cable news networks, is ignored or even applauded when a black person does the same thing. Humor and satire that have been acceptable for centuries when directed at white politicians become "hate" and "racism" when the target is a black or other non-white person. It doesn't make any sense, until you look at the big picture. When you do, you'll see that these non-stop accusations of racism are designed to intimidate and silence white people.

Think I'm exaggerating? How else to explain the uproar over the infamous Obama "Joker" poster that gripped the media in 2009? That summer, posters of Barack Obama began appearing mysteriously in cities all over America. The artist who designed the poster depicted Obama as the Joker, the evil genius played by the late Heath Ledger in the blockbuster movie "*The Dark Knight*," complete with his sinister makeup. At the bottom of the poster there was a single word: SOCIALISM. It was an ingenious and extremely compelling statement on Obama's big government policies.

Well, that's what any normal person would have thought, anyway. Even an honest liberal who disagreed with the message would have to admit that the unknown artist had tapped into and combined a couple of powerful social memes as few others have ever done in the world of politics. However, there aren't a whole lot of honest liberals these days, and none of the ones in the media were praising the artist for his talent and ingenuity. Instead, they were denouncing the poster as "mean spirited and dangerous" and, you guessed it, "racist" to boot. Earl Ofari Hutchinson, president of something called the Los Angeles Urban Policy Roundtable, and one of the most prominent critics of the poster, actually went so far as to demand that the creator of the anonymous poster identify himself: "We have issued a public challenge to the person or group that put up the poster to come forth and publicly tell why they have used this offensive depiction to ridicule President Obama."[15]

Wow. Since when do Americans have to answer to black journalists for their political opinions? I don't remember seeing that in the Constitution. So much for freedom of speech, huh? Many people have never heard of Earl Ofari Hutchinson, but the media loves to give airtime to this radical black activist. According to Wikipedia, "Hutchinson has written extensively on race and politics in the *Los Angeles Times*, *Newsday*, *Washington Post*, *Christian Science Monitor*, *Chicago Tribune*, and *Baltimore Sun*." He has made numerous appearances on national TV to talk about race and politics, and has been featured in *Time*, *Newsweek*, and the *New York Times*. You can certainly see why the media loves Hutchinson. Apparently all this media attention has gone to his head, and he now thinks he has the right to tell Americans what they can and can't say about a black president.

---

[15]http://www.ktla.com/news/landing/ktla-obama-posters,0,940643.story

Hutchinson wasn't the only person in the media to denounce the Obama Joker poster, not by a long shot. MSNBC showed a picture of the poster with the subtitle "Right Wing Hate?" below it.[16] The always reliably left-wing *Washington Post* allowed one of their writers to foam at the mouth at the outrageous idea that people should be free to lampoon Barack Hussein Obama. Philip Kennicott, who writes about art for the *Post*, wrote an unbelievably insane column about how "racist" the poster was.[17] Kennicott would appear to be completely unhinged, judging by this column. He started off by admitting that yes, people had been portraying George W. Bush the very same way long before the Obama "Joker" poster made the news. But that was entirely different, according to Kennicott. Why? Well, because Bush is white, and Obama is black. No, I'm not exaggerating. That's what the man said. Then he really lost all touch with reality. He went on to say that in the Batman movie, the Joker character represented people's fears of urban blacks and their criminal proclivities. Therefore, it's okay to show Bush as the Joker, but vicious racism to depict Obama in the exact same way.

Really? Let's see; the Joker was a white man in the movie. A white actor, Heath Ledger, played him. And this is how the director chose to play to the audience's allegedly racist fears about black crime? If you're having trouble wrapping your head around that concept, don't feel bad. It doesn't make a bit of sense to me, either. But apparently it makes perfect sense to liberals in the mainstream media. MSNBC even interviewed Kennicott about his column. And Kendicott didn't back down. He may be goofy as all get out, but at least he's consistent:

> "Well, I go back to the original context of the Joker in the Batman films. And these films have always been about urban fears, and quite simply, those fears code in many ways, black. They play into anti-African-American stereotypes."

[16]http://newsbusters.org/blogs/kyle-drennen/2009/08/06/msnbc-picks-wapo-article-claiming-obama-joker-poster-racist

[17]http://www.washingtonpost.com/wp-dyn/content/article/2009/08/05/AR2009080503876.html?hpid=artslot

The MSNBC interviewer then brought up the fact that liberals had made Joker posters about George Bush, and asked why is it racist to do the same thing to Obama? Kennicott patiently explained it to her, even though everyone should know without asking what's wrong with treating Obama the same way Bush was treated:

"Well, I mean, for the obvious reason that George Bush wasn't black. I mean in this case, I think what they're doing is finding an image that actually has undercurrents when applied to Obama that it simply didn't have when it applied to Bush."

And this guy actually gets paid to write for a major newspaper? And they wonder why newspapers are dying? Incredible. Kennicott went on to say that in every conversation Americans have about Obama, they're not just talking about politics, but also about race, so it's imperative therefore to examine every conservative position and argument for hidden racism. In other words, it doesn't matter what conservatives say about Obama (or other non-white politicians), liberals will always be able to examine it, hold it up to the light, and detect the "racism" that's driving it. That's a pretty neat trick. No need to worry about coming up with rebuttals or counter arguments when you're a liberal. You can just demonize conservatives as racists, and you win.

Don't make the mistake of thinking this is some sort of exception, that liberals and non-whites are just being ultra-sensitive because Obama is America's first non-white president, and that once he's been in office for a few years these attacks on conservatives who make fun of him will stop. That's what some conservatives have told me. Their argument goes something like this: "Sure, James, liberals and the media and racial lobbies are overreacting to what they perceive as being attacks on Obama, when we only intend to be humorous. They're reading racism into everything we say, no matter how innocent our intentions.

It's too bad, but given the situation, it's not unexpected, and frankly, it's hard to blame them. Once things have calmed down, things will get back to normal, and American politics will once again return to its rough and tumble spirit. Until then, we just need to sit back and avoid rocking the boat, so they can't paint us as a bunch of racists."

Well, with all due respect to my friends who feel this way, I can't stress enough how wrong they are. Not just wrong, but dangerously wrong. It's not a temporary measure at all that will go away once Obama has been around a while. No, it's only going to get worse. If we don't start fighting back now, and insisting on our right to ridicule, lampoon and laugh at any politician we disagree with, not just white ones, and in any way we see fit, then we'll not only lose our precious right of free speech, we'll also be rendered politically impotent. If the media and the Democrats and the racial lobbying groups can tell us what we can and can't say or write about Obama, by screaming *"Racism!"* whenever a conservative cracks a politically incorrect joke, or makes a funny drawing or altered photo of Obama, the game will be over, ladies and gentlemen. And it will be over for good.

That's what this is all about. It's not about civility, or manners, or raising the level of discourse, or whatever phony excuse liberals and the left-wing media come up with to justify their assaults on our free speech. It's about paralyzing conservatives by making us feel guilty and ashamed for disagreeing with a non-white politician. It's about getting us to second-guess ourselves constantly, always questioning our own motives, so instead of playing hardball politics and trying to win elections, we play softball and try to please the media, liberals and a powerful minority so they won't call us racists. And that, my friends, is not a winning program. It's time to say "No more Mr. Nice Guy," and start laughing in their faces when they call us racists. If we don't, we can forget ever rolling back the Obama revolution.

CHAPTER 6

Racism: It's Everywhere

Racism: it's a marvel of modern science. It's everywhere, just like oxygen and gravity and all sorts of other natural wonders. And just like those mysterious forces and substances, racism is practically invisible. But only to conservative white folks. Thankfully, Mother Nature has generously provided non-whites and liberals with special sensors that enable them to detect this insidious, invisible force everywhere it's found. And these days, it's literally found everywhere.

Racism is what's for breakfast, if you're white. And for lunch. And for dinner. And for dessert. And if you snack in between meals, those are no doubt racist snacks, too. I'm not sure if brushing your teeth has been declared racist yet, but it's probably best to avoid it, because if not, it's only a matter of time until the idea that white teeth are preferable to colored ones is officially condemned as hateful and racist.

Racism is pretty much every place you want to be, too, assuming you're white. It's at school (and the harder we try to eradicate it, the worse it gets.) It's at colleges and universities, too, even the "liberal" schools that brag about how "non-racist" they are. That's silly, of course. If a college or university is run by white people, it's racist. Period.

Racism is at home, too. No matter where you live, if you're white, it's a racist home in a racist neighborhood. If you're white and you move away from a black neighborhood, that's white flight, and that's some heavy-duty racism right there. Of course, if you're white, and you move from a white part of town into a black neighborhood, that's gentrification, and it's hard-core racism, too. It can be hard to keep up with all the rules, until you finally grasp the fact that when it comes to racism, there is only one rule: if you're white, you're a racist.

If you're white, racism is at your place of employment, too. Oh boy, is it ever at work! There is so much racism in the workplaces of America that it's a wonder any work gets done at all. Apparently white folks do nothing at work but two things: 1) sit around hating and discriminating against non-whites, and 2) sit around and dream up new ways to hate and discriminate against non-whites. Thankfully, though, we've got professionals in place to handle the problem, and they're doing an excellent job of it. In fact, they're constantly discovering new forms of racism and, whaddya know, these newfangled kinds of racism are always the fault of white folks, too.

How about when you're going to work? Are you racist then? Yes! It's an unfortunate fact of life that even racists have to get to work one way or another, and they'll keep doing so until that glorious day when all racists are fired from their jobs, rounded up and thrown in prison. All right-thinking people naturally look forward to that fast-approaching time with anticipation, but until it comes racists will be going to work, and how will they be doing it? *Racist-ly*, of course!

Until recently, most people probably didn't know that some ways of getting to work are "racist." But liberals and race hustlers have recently informed us that HOV lanes are now officially racist, too. That's right; HOV lanes are racist! When you and your carpool buddies drive in one, you can kid yourselves all you want that you're simply trying to reduce your use of gasoline and cut down on harmful emissions into the environment, but liberals and race hustlers know better - you and your carpool pals are just a lynch mob waiting to happen!'"[18]

This may seem shocking; but that's just because you haven't been paying attention. And do you know why you haven't been paying attention? It's because you're a racist! That's right, you're racist even when you're not thinking at all. Your life has been built on centuries of white privilege and racism, and you're reaping the benefits of it day in and day out, no matter if your best friend *really is* a black guy!

What's that? You're a blue-collar worker who has never had anything handed to him, and none of your ancestors owned slaves so you don't believe in white privilege and, even if there were such a thing, you're not benefiting from it? See? Right there! The very fact that you deny that you benefit from white privilege proves you're a no good racist, even if your racism is subconscious. Just for the record, though, most liberals and non-whites aren't buying your line. That whole "subconscious" thing is just a backup plan. They know for a fact that you're well aware of white privilege and how you benefit from it, and you're simply lying about it.

Of course, the more polite ones won't actually say "you're lying." They'll just say you're "in denial," which simply means you're lying to yourself before you lie to the world about not being racist. They just talk about it being "subconscious" so you can save face. Who wants to admit to being a flat-out liar, even if the whole world knows it? And when it comes to white folks who claim they're not racist, the whole world knows they're lying.

Do what now? You think that's crazy, and what about affirmative action, and racial set-asides in government contracts, and minority hiring quotas, and scholarships for non-whites only, and Miss Black America, and Black Entertainment Television, and the NAACP and the United Negro College Fund, and it doesn't make any sense to talk about white privilege with all

---

[18]http://boortz.com/nealz_nuze/2009/09/now-hov-lanes-are-racist.html

these programs and policies that punish people for being white and reward them for being black or Hispanic?

Wow, mister. You actually kiss your mother with that mouth?

I certainly hope you don't go around talking that way at work or in polite company, because no honorable person would ever think such thoughts, let alone utter them out loud. It's obvious to all good, decent people that affirmative action and quotas and set-asides and all the other efforts we make to supposedly correct past injustices in America, have actually done very little to address the problem of racism, and they have never inconvenienced or hindered or disadvantaged any white person in any way whatsoever.

Only a stone cold racist would complain about such paltry efforts to balance the scales, let alone complain that these programs are unjust in any way. Aren't you late for your Klan meeting, mister?

Just give it up, dude. You're a racist. If you doubt it, go look in the mirror. Are you white? Then you're a racist, and you really need to stop kidding yourself. Millions of white folks got the shock of their lives in 2008. They've been lifelong Democrats, supporting the party of Jesse Jackson and Al Sharpton, Jimmy Carter and Ted Kennedy. They even voted for Bill Clinton, who, up until quite recently, was known among black people as America's first black president. They thought they had every reason to be patting themselves on the back, because their racial bona fides were certainly in order. Imagine their surprise when they were informed by Obama supporters that Bill Clinton is a racist!

It must be pretty hard to pat yourself on the back when your head is spinning. Bill Clinton a racist? It's quite a jump from America's first black president to racist, especially when it happens overnight. But those who were shocked at this news simply hadn't been paying attention all these years. If they had, they would have known that Bill Clinton is, ipso facto, a racist. Uh, he's white? Helloooo? Hillary Clinton, being quite white herself, is also a confirmed racist. And all those white people who've been voting Democrat for decades? What part of "white Democrat" did you not understand? They're white, so they're racist. End of discussion.

Like I said a few paragraphs back, racism is everywhere, and it's invisible and insidious, and only non-whites and liberals can see it. Liberals can only see it in others, though; never in themselves. Why? Because they're white people, which means they're racists, and racists always deny their own racism!

Folks, you will never be able to understand politics and culture in today's America unless you grasp this fundamental truth at the root of more and more political and cultural battles in this country:

A racist is a white person.

Racist equals white person, and white person equals racist.

All white people are racist, and they're always racist, and they will always be racist.

Period.

Write that down in your day planner, make a note of it on your Blackberry or iPhone, put little sticky notes all over your house, or whatever you have to do until this message sinks in. Because until you grasp this, less and less of what's going on in this country will make any sense at all, and you'll be at the mercy of the liberal mainstream media, aggressive and hostile racial pressure groups, and white liberals (who are deluding themselves by thinking they're not racists.)

And once you do understand this fundamental truth of 21st century America, a whole bunch of things will suddenly start making sense. It will be like a light going off in your head, and suddenly everything will become clear. You'll understand exactly what is happening, and what is being done to you and your family and friends and neighbors. You'll understand for the first time why all your efforts at resisting liberalism and socialism in the past have come to nothing, and how you can finally start fighting back effectively. And it all begins by understanding one simple thing:

A racist is a white person.

Racist equals white person, and white person equals racist.

All white people are racist, and they're always racist, and they will always be racist.

It doesn't matter that you don't have a hateful bone in your body, or that you believe all people should be treated equally by the law, and civilly by their fellow man, no matter the color of his skin.

A racist is a white person.

Racist equals white person, and white person equals racist.

All white people are racist, and they're always racist, and they will always be racist.

It doesn't matter how many black friends you have.

A racist is a white person.

Racist equals white person, and white person equals racist.

All white people are racist, and they're always racist, and they will always be racist.

It doesn't matter how racially integrated your church is.

A racist is a white person.

Racist equals white person, and white person equals racist.

All white people are racist, and they're always racist, and they will always be racist.

It doesn't matter if you're a liberal or a conservative, a Democrat or a Republican.

A racist is a white person.

Racist equals white person, and white person equals racist.

All white people are racist, and they're always racist, and they will always be racist.

It doesn't matter how much money you've given to the NAACP or the United Negro College Fund.

A racist is a white person.

Racist equals white person, and white person equals racist.

All white people are racist, and they're always racist, and they will always be racist.

Got it? If not, don't worry. By the end of this book it will be crystal clear. After you're finished reading it, you may even be mentally beating yourself up, wondering how you could have missed this fundamental truth of modern-day America for all these years.

But don't feel bad; it's not necessary to berate yourself. Not one white person in a hundred understands this yet. The mainstream media and hate groups like the ADL, the SPLC, the NAACP, the Urban League, La Raza and countless others have masterfully disguised this fact, hiding it from the general public, lest they accidentally wake up the sleeping giant.

Few non-white agitators are so bold or careless as to state the truth as starkly and bluntly as I've put it. Every now and then a non-white hothead will let the truth slip out, but they will be ignored by the mainstream media, and they will then disappear down the memory hole, along with their statement, as if they simply never existed.

So it's hardly a surprise that most white people have no idea when they hear or see the word "racist" in the media that the people using the word mean something far different than what the ordinary person understands the word to mean. When the talking heads on the cable channels, or the famous bloggers, or the columnists for the dinosaur newspapers talk about those evil racists out there, the average white person thinks they understand what is being said or written, but they don't, because it hasn't yet dawned on them that "racist" has become code for "white."

Well, it's time we started understanding.

CHAPTER 7

Idiocracy....It's Not Just A Movie

Okay, kids, here we go. Strap on your seat belts, because the next few chapters are going to be a wild and woolly ride through the world of political correctness, lunatic liberalism, and the vicious double standard that is used to destroy white people who transgress one iota of the various dogmas, while giving a free pass to non-whites who commit much more heinous violations. Every example will provide us with a valuable lesson, and by the time we get to the end we'll see that these rules about "racism" have obviously been crafted with one goal in mind — to condemn whites as racists for pretty much anything and everything they do, while excusing virtually anything and everything non-whites do, no matter how egregious.

So let's get down to the nitty gritty, shall we? For instance, you may have noti—...

Oh, crap... Did I actually say nitty gritty? Looks like I did. I can't believe it! Wouldn't ya know it? I start off writing one of the main chapters in a book about racism, and I accidentally use a racist phrase to kick it off. Boy, is my face red! Yes, most people probably aren't aware of it yet, but "nitty gritty" is now on the list of hateful, racist words that decent people just don't say. It seems some politically correct egghead at some PC university allegedly "discovered" ("made up" is more like it) that nitty gritty is what the crews of slave ships used to call the debris found at the bottom of the ship after carrying a shipload of slaves to America to be sold.

As far as I know, this has never been proven. It seems to me that if it were true, we would have heard about it a long, long time ago. In fact, we probably never would've heard the end of it. And even if it is true, so what? Who in their right mind would care about such a thing? Are we supposed to know the history and etymology of every word we ever use? That's ridiculous. We all use thousands of words every year (OK, maybe not Al Sharpton, whose vocabulary is probably in the low hundreds), and there is no way to trace the history of every single one of them and make sure they never had any connection to anything unsavory in the past.

And even if they did have some unsavory or "racist" meaning or connotation in the past, what's the big deal? Words and cultures evolve over centuries, and many words today have traveled a long way from their original meanings. The word "girl" used to mean any prepubescent child of either sex. "Deer" used to refer to any four-legged animal. When people talk about their plans for next Thursday, do they really believe the 5th day of the week belongs to Thor? How about Saturday? Do people who use that word really believe it's Saturn's day? No, that's silly, and we all would recognize how silly someone was being if they insisted that everyone who uses those words is using them in their original sense.

Atheists tell people goodbye all the time, yet the word is literally nothing but a contraction of "God be with ye." So do atheists secretly believe in God? That's absurd. And it's just as absurd to say that the use of the words "nitty gritty" is racist. That's what we're told, though. In fact, over in Great Britain "nitty gritty" is on an official list of "racist" words and phrases police officers aren't allowed to say.[19] The United Kingdom is just a few years ahead of the United States on the road to a state of totalitarian political correctness, so don't think that what happens over there isn't relevant. It will be happening soon enough here in America, if it hasn't already happened. You can count on it.

Besides, anyone who thinks it's not already that crazy here in America simply has no idea what's going on out there these days. This kind of stuff is way out of control here in "the land of the free," and it has been for quite some time. Have you ever seen the movie called "Idiocracy"? If you haven't, you should go rent it as soon as possible. It's set some 500 years in the future in America, which has literally become a nation of idiots. Of course, Mike Judge, the director of the movie, had to tone things down or his movie would never have seen the light of day. In the movie, for example, the population of America is still a white majority, by a large margin. That's not realistic at all. Already, half the babies being born in this country are non-white, and in just a few years, white people will make up less than half the total population. I'm sure Mike Judge, who created "King of the Hill" and "Beavis and Butthead," is well aware of these trends, and he knows that the idea that America will still be majority white 500 years from now is ludicrous. But he also knew that there wasn't a snowball's chance in you-know-where of getting his movie made and released if it had been about an America 500 years from now full of nothing but idiots, and those idiots are mostly black and brown. It would have been buried forever, and he would probably never work in Hollywood again. Even as sanitized as it was, the movie company only allowed it to be shown on a tiny number of screens.

Needless to say, even though it's a comedy, "Idiocracy" is a depressing movie. What's even more depressing is that in many ways, we're already living in a version of the nightmare of stupidity the movie depicts. It may be funny as a dark comedy

---

[19]http://news.bbc.co.uk/2/hi/uk_news/politics/1988681.stm

set 500 years in the future, but when it's starting to happen to us in real life, and it just gets worse with every passing week, month and year, it's not the least bit amusing. We're allowing the least intelligent among us to use political correctness (and the ever-present but unmentioned threat of riots) to dictate what we can and can't do, say, or even think. And every day, the straitjacket we've allowed them to strap us into gets tighter and tighter. We're not yet a nation made up of nothing but idiots, but we're increasingly ruled by idiots, which is what "idiocracy" means. The average race hustler or "civil rights activist" is not exactly Ivy League material, to put it mildly. For example, listen to Al Sharpton's radio show — he can't even pronounce the word "ask," for crying out loud. Low IQ, combined with hypersensitivity in the same person or group, is a deadly combination when it comes to free thought and free speech, yet it is precisely these people and groups who are increasingly exercising veto power over what we can think, say and do.

Haven't we lost enough of our freedoms in the name of civil rights? Freedom of association, the right to decide who is allowed on your own property and who isn't, and the right to hire and fire people as we see fit....these and other freedoms were taken away a long time ago in the name of Equality. Now, free speech in America is just hanging by a thread, and if we don't start fighting back immediately, it will soon be a thing of the past, just like freedom of association and the other precious freedoms which were, at one time, the birthright of all Americans. I hate to sound like a broken record, but if you think I'm exaggerating, or just being overly dramatic, well you simply haven't been paying attention. Just keep reading. You'll not only be convinced, you'll be angry when you realize what hostile minority groups, the liberal media, and the forces of political correctness are doing to the right of free speech by turning every little thing that upsets any black or other non-white person into "racism" or "hate," no matter how ludicrous or insane.

To be fair, maybe I shouldn't paint the situation with so broad a brush. It's not that all "offended" blacks and other "oppressed" groups are deliberately out to trample on our free speech rights. No, often when they scream *"Racism!"* they're doing it with a simple and straightforward intention — to get money from the white man. Black people especially are taught from the time they come out of the womb that they're victims of the evil white man, and that we owe them. Big time. They hear it from their parents (or, more accurately, their mother, as Dad is usually nowhere in the vicinity). They hear it eight hours a day in school. They hear it from their churches, where a thousand Jeremiah Wrights preach hatred of whitey every Sunday. And there is no way to measure how often they hear it from the mainstream media, because that message is so prevalent on TV (and blacks in America watch more TV than any other racial group.) Millions of them absorb these messages until it becomes second nature. They believe white people are evil and wish them harm. Furthermore, they believe their own "civil rights" trump the constitutional rights of white people, because "racists" shouldn't have any rights. It naturally follows that they should always be suspicious of everything white people say or do, and anything they find offensive in any way entitles them to make demands for apologies, money, or other forms of redress.

In other words, every interaction a white person has with a black person these days is pretty much a lawsuit just waiting to happen. Like the one that "happened" to Southwest Airlines a few years ago over a flight attendant asking people to find a seat quickly so the plane could take off. As most people are aware, Southwest has long prided itself on not being a "typical" airline. When it first started a few decades ago, the flight attendants wore hot pants, for example. Until recently, there were no assigned seats on their flights. Southwest has always tried to create an image of a laid back, fun-loving airline, in contrast to their stuffy, old fashioned competitors. Their marketing strategy has been very successful. Even though it was always a "no frills" airline, Southwest became quite popular in a short time. Their flight attendants were loved for their carefree, often whimsical ways of interacting with passengers.

Until they became famous overnight for their "racist" instructions to passengers, that is. Yes, a couple of black passengers sued Southwest Airlines for racism, and the case wound up dragging through the courts for months; years with appeals. What happened? Well, as I mentioned, at the time of the incident, Southwest didn't have assigned seating. It was first come, first served, and if the plane wasn't full, people would often take a long time to pick a seat, or they would keep moving to one they thought was better. That was the case on this day, and takeoff time was rapidly approaching, so everyone needed to be in a seat with their safety belt on. So the flight attendant got on the intercom and said "Eeny meeny miny mo, pick a seat we gotta go." Pretty heinous, huh? Well, for any sane person it's hard to see how anyone could have been harmed by this, but yes, reciting part of an ancient children's nursery rhyme actually led to a federal lawsuit for "racism."

The basis of the lawsuit was that the two black passengers who sued were "humiliated," because a variation of the actual nursery rhyme, instead of saying "catch a tiger by the toe," instead says "catch a n**ger by the toe," and therefore what most people thought was actually a lighthearted ditty by the flight attendant was actually a hate-fueled racist assault on these two passengers. One of the plaintiffs claimed she was so upset at the "racism" that she suffered repeated seizures after the remark, and wound up being bedridden for three days because of the "incident."[20]

Never mind that the flight attendant, Jennifer Cunditt, was a young lady in her early 20s who swore up and down that, not only did she bear no ill will toward blacks at all, but she had never even heard the alternate version of the nursery rhyme. Which was entirely believable — millions of people had never heard it, even back in the bad old days before Martin Luther King, Jr., and the verse's already-limited popularity had died down quite a bit after the civil rights revolution. (It may be hard to believe for anyone who went to public school, or watches too much TV, but pre-MLK America wasn't filled with tens of millions of white parents teaching their kids to hate blacks or use "the N-word," not even in the South.)

But none of that mattered. See, unfortunately for Jennifer Cunditt, she was white, and she worked for a major airline which is seen as part of the "white establishment," and a couple of the passengers on that fateful (hateful?) flight were black. It didn't matter how many times the flight attendant swore up and down she wasn't a racist. She's white, and all white people are "racists," white people are always out to harm blacks, and black peoples' feelings trump the so-called "rights" of racists. Ipso facto, the airline owed the black people money. So they went to court to get what was rightfully theirs.

Eventually, they lost their case. So, sadly, the "dream is still deferred," blah blah blah. But what's important is that they weren't laughed out of court the day they filed the lawsuit. The fact that any attorney would take this case is shocking enough; that the judge didn't throw the plaintiffs out on their ears and threaten their attorney with contempt charges for filing a frivolous lawsuit is even more outrageous. It's actually much worse than that — according to *USA Today*, they didn't hire a lawyer; the court appointed them an attorney after they filed a handwritten complaint![21] Of course, you can guess why they lost the case in the end. Yep, that ol' debbil racism. There were no blacks on the jury, which meant they couldn't get justice. One of the plaintiffs stated:

"If we had jurors of our peers then we would have won the case today, and we should have won the case today, with all the evidence shown. It's a shame that the jury pool we had to draw from did not have one black and not one minority. Something has to be done to make sure there is justice in America for blacks."[22]

Why can't black people get justice from an all white jury? Because, in the eyes of the media, the PC lobby, and the vast majority of non-whites in this country, all white people are

---

[21]http://www.usatoday.com/travel/news/2004-01-22-swa-rhyme_x.htm
[22]http://www.usatoday.com/travel/news/2004-01-22-swa-rhyme_x.htm

racists. And the fact that any white person would even try to argue this point is simply further evidence of their racism. While the plaintiffs didn't hit the hoped-for jackpot, they did manage it to give a little payback to whitey. There is no telling how many hundreds of thousands of dollars Southwest Airlines had to pay in legal fees, and that's hardly the end of the story. How many people heard on the news that Southwest was accused of racism, and without hearing the absurd details, decided the company really is racist? In an idiocracy, one news story, no matter how biased or slanted, can ruin a person or a company. What about poor Jennifer Cunditt? Many people who didn't hear all the facts probably assumed that she had done something pretty terrible to wind up at the center of a lawsuit over racial discrimination. After all, most people don't think we live in the kind of country where you can be dragged into court and have your reputation smeared or ruined, and be saddled with huge legal fees, simply for saying "eeny meeny miny mo." But that's life in an idiocracy.

And Jennifer Cunditt is not the only person in America to have her life turned upside down over the phrase "eeny meeny miny mo." Yes, believe it or not, the Southwest Airlines case was not an isolated incident. In University City, Missouri, near St. Louis, a white woman named Eileen Duggan went through an even worse nightmare over the phrase. Duggan was Public Relations Director for University City. Every year the city would put out an events calendar and send copies out to the community, and one of Duggan's jobs was to coordinate production of the calendar. The 2002 calendar featured a photo on the cover of little kids' feet in a circle, some with shoes, and some barefoot, with a finger touching one of the feet. The caption, of course, was "Eeny Meeny Miny Moe." For the record, the photographer was a black woman, and she also wrote the caption. But before the calendar even hit the streets, Duggan was getting calls from blacks who were "outraged" at the hideous "racism" depicted in the cover photo.

The next thing she knew, a local hate whitey "civil rights

activist" calling himself Anthony Shahid was on the radio denouncing the picture, especially a white tennis shoe in it, which he said was intended to celebrate the white man's oppression of the black race.[23] Then Shahid began confronting the mayor of University City who, instead of telling the simpleton to get the hell out of his office and get a job, quickly gave in to the intimidation tactics and blocked the calendar from being distributed any further. The city then paid some $14,000 to have the calendar reprinted with a new "non-racist" cover photo. But that wasn't enough to satisfy Shahid. He wanted a white scalp, and he was going to raise Cain until he got one. He demanded the mayor fire PR Director Duggan, who, even though she hadn't taken the picture or written the caption, was white, and therefore was a racist. He and his simple minded followers picketed City Hall and tied up the phone lines for days until the mayor once again gave in and fired Eileen Duggan.[24]

Eileen Duggan was fired for doing nothing wrong. Over a photograph that was taken and captioned by a black woman, and which most people thought was a sweet and touching homage to childhood innocence. But that's life in Idiocracy, where low-IQ thugs can ruin someone's life by rounding up even more simple-tons and "making demands" until the powers that be give in, out of fear of riots, or worse. Eileen Duggan was fired for being white, the worst crime you can commit in modern America.

If blacks get so bent out of shape over a children's nursery rhyme, you can just imagine how they're going to react when a reference to a scientific fact is made. Well, there is no need to waste time trying to imagine it; all you have to do is live in Dallas, Texas, where this next story took place. This one is even more unbelievable, because it involves not just private citizens who are outraged over their ignorance, but elected officials. One is even a judge, for crying out loud. A lot of people who aren't aware of this story may find it hard to believe. Well, check the footnotes, because it's one hundred percent true.

---

[23]http://www.riverfronttimes.com/2003-02-19/news/who-s-afraid-of-anthony-shahid/6
[24]http://www.mail-archive.com/volokh-1@lists.ucla.edu/msg00891.html

It happened in July of 2008, during a meeting of the Dallas County Commissioners.[25] They were discussing a huge problem that citizens were reporting with the collections office, which keeps track of traffic tickets and payments for those tickets in some Dallas courts. Or, at least the office is supposed to keep track of these things, but it wasn't happening. Lots of people weren't being notified of court appearance dates, fines that were paid weren't getting processed, etc., and the problem was getting out of hand.

Kenneth Mayfield, one of the white County Commissioners at the meeting, said, "It sounds like Central Collections has become a black hole." Now, pretty much anyone in America who has made it past fourth grade on their own merits knows exactly what a black hole is, and the metaphor was quite appropriate. Just as with a black hole, things were being sucked into Central Collections and were never seen again.

Not every adult in America got past fourth grade on their own merits though, and one of them is evidently Dallas County Commissioner John Wiley Price. John Wiley Price is black, and he was "outraged" over Kenneth Mayfield's "racist" remark. "Excuse me?! Excuse me?! Call it a white hole!"

No, I'm not making this up. (To watch the video for yourself, go to YouTube and put in "John Wiley Price black hole.") An elected official in 21st-century America actually didn't know the meaning of a black hole, and thought it was a racist remark. If that wasn't bad enough, a black judge who was at the meeting then interrupted the proceedings and demanded an apology in an "aggrieved" voice. Judge Thomas Jones makes those women on that Southwest Airlines flight look like Rhodes Scholars:

"Could I get an apology from the commissioner ? In this day and time you don't sit around a table where you have diversity and refer to a black hole."[26]

Wow. You don't use the term "black hole" in front of

[25]http://cityhallblog.dallasnews.com/archives/2008/07/dallas-county-meeting-turns-ra.html
[26]http://www.youtube.com/watch?v=oc1zGRUPztc

diversity? No, you'd better not use any words a first grader wouldn't understand when you have "diversity at the table," or you'll probably be called a racist. Incredible. They say ignorance is bliss. If that's true, Dallas County Justice of the Peace Thomas Jones and County Commissioner John Wiley Price must be two of the happiest men in America.

The appalling ignorance displayed by these two buffoons is bad enough. What's really appalling, though, is that America is supposed to be an advanced country, and yet people like John Wiley Price actually get elected County Commissioner, and Thomas Jones is allowed to be a judge. These clowns shouldn't even have a high school diploma, but thanks to affirmative action, racial quotas, "voting rights" decisions and political correctness they're actually in positions of authority, making decisions that impact people's lives. And not only do they not even know what a black hole is, they actually think it's a racist term? How is any self-respecting person supposed to look at Thomas Jones and call him "Your Honor?" Every American should be outraged and disgusted that illiterates like this, of any race, are even allowed to run for office, let alone actually hold one.

When that story came out, there was a lot of mocking and eye rolling in the conservative blogosphere, but that's about it. Mainstream conservatives see this sort of thing as a source of humor, but they stop there, which is a big mistake. Now, there's no denying that it is quite a spectacle to see two elected officials in America make it clear for all to see that they're complete simpletons. If it were just an isolated incident, it really would be funny. In fact, this scene could have come right out of *Idiocracy*. It's not an isolated incident, though. Not by any stretch of the imagination. It is part of a widespread and growing trend, and instead of being amused, we should be horrified at what this portends for America's future. Elected officials like John Wiley Price and "Judge" Thomas Jones will only become more numerous in our increasingly multiracial America.

What else would you expect in a nation where courts can

be tied up in litigation over "civil rights" violations involving a nonsensical kids' nursery rhyme? A nation where the computer terms "master drive" and "slave drive," which have been used for decades, have to be changed because they're "offensive"?[27] Yes, this actually happened, too. It seems that a black employee in the Los Angeles County Probation Office saw a master drive and a slave drive on a piece of equipment, and actually filed a "discrimination" complaint with the Affirmative Action board. So something had to be done. One moron gets "offended" because they're too stupid to understand something, and everything must be changed to accommodate their ignorance. Because you simply can't tell a moron to get a library card and stop being a moron; not if they're non-white. Here's the memo from the Los Angeles County Purchasing Department:

"Subject: IDENTIFICATION   OF   EQUIPMENT
                    SOLD TO LA COUNTY
Date: Tue, 18 Nov 2003 14:21:16 -0800
From: 'Los Angeles County'

The County of Los Angeles actively promotes and is committed to ensure a work environment that is free from any discriminatory influence be it actual or perceived. As such, it is the County's expectation that our manufacturers, suppliers and contractors make a concentrated effort to ensure that any equipment, supplies or services that are provided to County departments do not possess or portray an image that may be construed as offensive or defamatory in nature.

One such recent example included the manufacturer's labeling of equipment where the words "Master/Slave" appeared to identify the primary and secondary sources. Based on the cultural diversity and sensitivity of Los Angeles County, this is not an acceptable identification label.

---

[27]http://www.snopes.com/inboxer/outrage/master.asp

We would request that each manufacturer, supplier and contractor review, identify and remove/change any identification or labeling of equipment or components thereof that could be interpreted as discriminatory or offensive in nature before such equipment is sold or otherwise provided to any County department.

Thank you in advance for your cooperation and assistance.

> Joe Sandoval, Division Manager
> Purchasing and Contract Services
> Internal Services Department
> County of Los Angeles"

Makes ya proud to be an American, doesn't it?

Well, if that doesn't, maybe this story will. While I was writing this book, I was confronted with so many examples of members and leaders of a supposedly advanced, civilized nation groveling and apologizing to the unbelievably ignorant for their ignorance, that I could have written three entire books on this topic alone. Needless to say, the competition for the most outrageously stupid complaint of "racism" was tough, and it would be impossible to pick a winner. (Besides, next week will no doubt bring an even more ludicrous complaint of "racism." If you ever lack for reading material, just set up a news alert for "racism," "racist," etc.; and your e-mail in box will be flooded.) But if I had to settle on just one story, it would have been either the Eeny Meeny Miny Mo/Southwest Airlines affair, or this next one, which took place in Columbus, Georgia.

The occasion was a "civil rights" celebration/protest/march/riot or whatever on Martin Luther King, Jr. Day, 2005. As busloads of black people headed into the city for the event, they were greeted by police officers directing traffic. So far, so good, right? I mean, anytime a crowd of any size it's expected, it's perfectly normal to send cops out to direct traffic in the area. But it wasn't the fact that police officers were out directing the traffic that caused the problem. No, it's what they were doing while they directed traffic in the vicinity of the "civil rights" event that caused such an uproar in the coming days.

Were they giving black people the finger? No.

Yelling death threats? No.

Screaming racial slurs at the busloads of black people? No.

Were they passing out KKK literature to passerby? No.

No, it was nothing like that.

It seems some of them were (and I hope you're sitting down) eating bananas.

James, you can't be serious? Yes I can be serious. It's the one-hundred-percent-honest-to-God truth. After the event, a black bus rider by the name of Gwen Stewart contacted the mayor of Columbus, GA, Robert Poydasheff, to actually raise hell about a cop eating a banana while on duty. She said she was deeply offended at this "affront," and evidently could not believe that in this day and age police officers would dare eat bananas in front of black people.[28] Apparently Gwen Stewart, like white liberals, thinks that "monkey" equals "black person," and has taken this theory to its next logical step. If "monkey" equal "black person," and all references to any kind of primate by a white person is actually secret racist code intended to demean blacks, it naturally follows that "bananas" are verboten, too. After all, don't monkeys and apes and chimps and orangutans eat bananas? So what else is it but racism when a white person eats a banana? Sure, it's theoretically possible that a white person might be eating a banana because he likes them, or he's trying to eat healthier, but in the eyes of many blacks (and all liberals) all white people are racist, so the most likely explanation is that the cops were eating the bananas to imply that black people are monkeys or something.

It must have been horrible for Gwen Stewart to be on that bus in Columbus, Georgia on Martin Luther King, Jr. Day 2005. Imagine the unspeakable terror she must have felt. Here it is, forty years after the Civil Rights Act became the law of the land,

---

[28]http://www.vdare.com/epstein/080417_obama.htm

and absolutely nothing has changed. Even on Martin Luther King, Jr. Day, the holiest day on the calendar, Jim Crow and Bull Connor are still alive and well! Well, okay, maybe one thing had changed — Bull Connor no longer uses water hoses and German Shepherds, and is now eating bananas to threaten and intimidate black folks, but other than that, it was just like the Freedom Rides of the 1960s. I can't imagine what a horrific experience it must have been for her. But the Civil Rights movement has certainly come a long way in fifty years.

We shall overcome!

I have a dream!

If the gloves don't fit you must acquit!

ARE YOU EATING A *&%(#$* BANANA?!?!

(Again, at the risk of sounding like a broken record, is it any wonder we have county commissioners like John Wiley Price and judges like Thomas Jones in this country?)

But once again, that's only half the story. Here's the kicker... the mayor of Columbus, Georgia, Robert Poydasheff, actually wrote a letter of apology to Gwen Stewart!

He not only apologized for police officers eating bananas, he also promised her it would never happen again!

Here's his letter:[29]

"Dear Ms. Stewart,

"I am sorry you found Columbus police officers eating bananas on the street when you arrived in Columbus for the protest. Let me assure you there was no intent to offend. The officers needed some nutrition after standing long hours on the street, and they particularly needed the potassium available in bananas and some other fruits.

"Accordingly, they were given bananas along with some drinking water. There was no thought of insulting or

---

[29]http://harpers.org/archive/2006/05/0081017

offending anyone, and perhaps that was thoughtless on our part. In any case, let me offer my sincere apology for anything our officers may have done that gave offense to you or anyone else. I want to assure you that it will not happen again. I want to encourage you to come back to Columbus and get to know us better. You will find this a place where African-Americans and all other people are valued equally and are welcomed to full participation in community life.

"Again, I am sorry you were offended, and I hope you will accept this sincere apology.

"Respectfully,

"Robert S. Poydasheff"

In-freakin'-credible. This guy should get some kind of award for the Most Spineless Politician of the Millennium. He makes John McCain look like Davy Crockett at the Alamo.

Can you believe the pathetic groveling in this letter from a mayor of an American city?

Not "Hey lady, what rock did you crawl out from under?"

or "I can't believe someone's mind could so twisted by hatred of white people that they could actually be offended at the sight of a banana."

or "If the police officers actually had been comparing you to a monkey, I would demand that they apologize to monkeys."

What has this country come to when an American mayor promises someone that he will make sure that no cops ever eat a banana on duty again so she will never again have to deal with the "affront" it caused her?

This is the country that fought for and achieved our independence from the greatest military power of the day, carved a nation out of the wilderness, won two World Wars, and put a man on the moon? And we're reduced to this? How in God's name does anyone think we're going to stand up to the radical socialists and multiculturalists when we drop to our knees and whimper out a craven apology the minute a minority claims to be offended by the sight of eating a banana? And never mind standing up to the terrorists among us...God help us.

CHAPTER 8

Nobody's Talking About Racism?

In her book *Guilty*, the incomparable Ann Coulter shows how liberals, especially medial liberals, love to praise themselves for their "courage" for being the only people with the guts to talk about what thousands of other liberals are babbling about pretty much non-stop. And she wrote that long before black CNN anchor Don Lemon found the "courage" to say this on national TV in September of 2009:

> "A member of Congress calling the President a liar, town-hallers yelling at lawmakers, carrying guns to rallies, refusing to let kids hear the Commander-in-Chief. And on and on and on. What's behind it? Is it racial? Yeah, I said it. And we're going to talk about it I was watching Real Talk, Real Time with Bill Maher and I was, like, 'Finally, someone's talking about this. Finally, someone is talking about this.'"[30]

---

[30]http://newsbusters.org/blogs/brent-baker/2009/09/13/cnns-lemon-praises-maher-raising-anti-obama-racism-finally-someones-tal

Finally! At long last someone had the guts to accuse people who disagree with Obama of being racists!

Yeah, like "finally" Al Gore has decided to end his silence and speak out against "global warming"...

Also in 2009, Democrats "finally" started criticizing President Bush's response to Hurricane Katrina.

I'm not sure where Don Lemon was during 2007 and 2008, but his pals in the media have been telling us that opposition to Obama was rooted in racism for years now. In fact, almost exactly a year before Lemon made his lunatic pronouncement, his fellow CNN anchor Jack Cafferty said that if Obama lost the upcoming election, it could only be due to racism. And notice how Cafferty himself makes the ridiculous claim that "nobody" is talking about the racial angle in the 2008 election:

> "Will race be the factor that keeps Obama from the White House? Race is arguably the biggest issue in this election, and it's one that nobody's talking about.
>
> The differences between Barack Obama and John McCain couldn't be more well defined. Obama wants to change Washington. McCain is a part of Washington and a part of the Bush legacy. Yet the polls remain close. Doesn't make sense...unless it's race.
>
> *Time* magazine's Michael Grunwald says race is the elephant in the room. He says Barack Obama needs to tread lightly as he fights back against the McCain-Palin campaign attacks."[31]

Yeah, Jack, "nobody" was talking about race and Obama in September 2008, if by "nobody" you mean everyone in the media pretty much 24 hours a day, 7 days a week. How can these guys write and say these things with a straight face? You'd think they'd be embarrassed, but apparently one of the requirements for working in the media is lacking a sense of shame (as well as not having a brain or a spine). And just what were all these

---

[31]http://politicalticker.blogs.cnn.com/2008/09/16/cafferty-obama-race-a-factor/

"attacks" coming from John McCain? If there was one thing McCain didn't do during his run for the presidency, it was go on the attack. Oh yeah, wait a minute...I think once McCain actually called Obama a liberal, which was obviously nothing but code word for "Negro" to inject race into the campaign and rile up the tens of millions of Kluxers out there in flyover land. (Which no one was talking about!)

Not only were the media furiously beating the "race" and "racism" horse even as Cafferty claimed no one was talking about it, they had been doing so from the minute Obama threw his hat into the ring in Springfield, Illinois all the way back in February of 2007. It was one of the first things mentioned in many articles and reports about Obama's electoral prospects. The notion that a professed journalist could boldly claim that "nobody" in the media had been talking about Obama, race and the election is so stupid that it boggles the mind. But that hasn't stopped "professional journalists" like Jack Cafferty and Don Lemon and many others from making this ridiculous claim. The idea that "nobody was talking about race and Obama" is way past being ridiculous; it's laughably absurd. Just for one example, *Time* magazine's politics blog on April 11, 2007, ran a piece about it. It's even titled *Obama, Race, and The Election*, for crying out loud.[32]

Here's another item from May of 2007. On the ABC political discussion program "*This Week*," Sam Donaldson, George Will, Cokie Roberts and George Stephanopoulus are discussing the fact that Obama is black, and that white "racism" will be a factor in his run for the White House, and the only question is how big of a negative factor "racism" will be:[33]

> *Sam Donaldson:* "You raised something, let's just put on the table: He's an African-American. Is the country ready? Well, I think it is. And he said he thinks it is. He said he thinks he'll lose some votes because of that, and

[32]http://realclearpolitics.blogs.time.com/2007/04/11/obama_race_and_the_election/
[33]http://newsbusters.org/node/12736

so the question is what does the word 'some' mean? In critical elections, not just in the South, it may mean some-thing."

Cokie Roberts: "Well sure. And it could be huge."

Yeah, absolutely nobody was talking about "racism" and Obama until Cafferty finally risked his career and bravely broke his silence. Good thing Jack Cafferty had the courage to finally bring it up right before the election, huh? Where would we be without Cafferty's groundbreaking analysis? I don't know about you, but when I think "fearless journalism," the first term that pops in my head is CNN. And since Jack Cafferty and Sam Roberts and Cokie Roberts are all officially non-racist, I don't think any of us have to wonder who any of them voted for in 2008. (In all fairness to Donaldson, though, he voted for Obama because he was worried McCain might crack down on the importation of cheap Chinese hairpieces.)

Now, there's no point in listing every single discussion of "racism" and Obama that took place in the national media prior to his election to the White House. Unless you were living under a rock for nearly two years, you certainly haven't forgotten the countless times that the media brought up the idea that race was going to be a significant hurdle for Obama to overcome, because of the tens of millions of white racists out there in flyover land. Countless is probably an understatement, in fact. On top of that, we were subjected to one report or article after another suggesting that if Obama didn't win, "racism" would be the only reason.

The media just loved to accuse white Americans of being so filled with "hate" and "racism" that they would never vote for Obama, or any black person running for president. In fact, many of their stories and reports focused on what has become known as the Bradley Effect, where a black candidate's actual votes from white people are far lower than pre-election polling would have predicted. In other words, many white people tell pollsters they're going to vote for a black candidate, but end up voting against him. It's named after Tom Bradley, the black mayor of Los Angeles, who ran for governor of California in 1982. Many polls showed him leading, but he wound up losing to the GOP candidate, and his percentage of the white vote wasn't nearly as high as the percentage of whites who said they planned to vote for him. The theory is that many white people are ashamed of their "racism," so they lie to pollsters because they don't want to seem "prejudiced," etc.

If you're bored sometime, go to Google and put in "Obama Bradley effect" (without the quotation marks) and see for yourself just how many pieces come up. Last time I looked, it was nearly 900,000. And this was from a time when supposedly "nobody was talking" about Obama, race, and the election. (Gosh, I wonder why so many people don't trust the media...?) Many of these stories were filed after Obama lost the New Hampshire Democratic primary to Hillary Clinton.[34] There was a lot of hand-wringing about "white racism" after that contest, because nearly all the polls showed Obama with a strong lead. Obama was on a roll, having just won Iowa, and New Hampshire was expected to fall in line. But it didn't. The theory was that in New Hampshire, actual ballots are used, whereas in Iowa the primary was a caucus format, which meant that everyone in the room knew where you stood. White Iowans were more likely to support Obama so they wouldn't look "racist" to others, but white people in New Hampshire didn't have to worry about that, because they voted in secret.

Now, don't get me wrong; I'm not denying the existence of the Bradley Effect. It most definitely does exist, which should hardly come as a surprise to anyone. Yes, believe it or not, after only fifty years of non-stop ranting, moralizing, pontificating, browbeating, name-calling, condemnation and brainwashing by the media that they're horrible, evil racists, some white people have actually come to believe it. Millions of them in fact. And even the ones who have successfully resisted internalizing this

---

[34] http://www.thenation.com/blogs/state_of_change/268328

self-hatred are always walking on eggshells in order to avoid being "perceived" as racists. They also know that pollsters (who, like most Americans, are usually white people), live in this same matrix, and are likely to interpret their vote against a black man as "racism," since non-white politicians in the media are almost always portrayed as brilliant, wise, compassionate and benevolent. What possible reason could a white person come up with that would justify voting against a saintly black person, and instead voting for an evil racist honky? So, in many cases, they don't even bother trying. They just lie and tell the person doing the polling that they're voting for the black guy. That way they don't have to deal with the shame that would ensue from admitting to be a "racist."

The Bradley Effect is just the tip of the iceberg, in fact. Our churches, schools and the media love to go on about how white racism is always bubbling up just below the surface, just waiting for any excuse to boil over into a hate-filled rage. Even if evil racist white folks somehow manage to resist their never-ending urges to start organizing lynching parties, the non-stop racism in our hearts is always there, and it always manages to work its way out and harm non-whites, even when we don't consciously mean for it to do so. Heck, shows like that can be seen pretty much any night of the week on PBS. Unless it's fund-raising week, when they feature things like concerts by Celtic Woman in order to get money out of those hateful racist white folks they spend the rest of the year demonizing.

Naturally, the situation is pretty much the opposite of the way it's portrayed in the media. That's always the case when it comes to race in the media; everything is turned upside down, and it's not an accident. Tune in any crime drama, and what do you see? You'll see affluent white people committing one heinous murder after another, and often their victims are non-whites. Yet when you watch the news, which reflects real life and not the hate-filled, poisonous fantasies of Hollywood liberals, affluent white killers are extremely rare, and white people of any class rarely kill non-whites. When they do, it's non-stop nationwide news, and ten years later it's still news, like in the James Byrd dragging murder. Blacks and Hispanics commit a greatly disproportionate share of violent crimes, and they often choose white people as victims, but you'd never know it from watching *Law & Order*, *CSI*, or any other Hollywood production.

No, white people aren't filled with hate and "racism;" but they are scared to death of being "perceived" as a racist, or getting called one, because "racist" has become the most powerful racial slur in America. Calling someone the N-word won't damage a person, but calling someone a racist can destroy their career overnight. Just ask Don Imus or Jimmy "The Greek" Snyder or Al Campanis, or a whole host of other white people whose lives have been ruined after the slur of "racist" was hurled at them. Nothing a black person says about race, no matter how outrageous or blatantly hateful ever seems to have a negative impact on their careers, but one slip of the tongue by a white person and they're treated like the incarnation of Satan.

So it's not white people's "racism" that's always there, just under the surface. It's their fear of being seen as a racist, or getting called one, that is constantly on their mind. This fear is so strong and so pervasive that many white people are even afraid to disagree with a black person in public. Radio talk show host Dennis Prager wrote about this phenomenon a few years ago in a column that's published online, which discussed his experience watching a focus group in action.[35]

If you're unfamiliar with the concept of focus groups, they're a common tool used by companies and other groups, such as political campaigns. A group of people is brought together and shown a new product, or an idea for a new TV show, or they might look at a couple of proposed ads for a politician or a product, to see which one is more effective. It's a way to test something to see how it will fly before rolling it out to the general public, or to get feedback on what improvements folks would like to see.

Prager was observing a focus group about talk radio. One

---

[35] http://www.realclearpolitics.com/articles/2006/07/how_liberals_injure_blacks.html

thing struck him as odd; there were only white people in the group. (I'm not sure what's so odd about that myself, since the overwhelming majority of political radio talk shows are conservative, and few black people are politically conservative, no matter what your preacher tells you.) Prager asked the marketers why no blacks were included. They told him that focus groups used to have both blacks and whites, but that's no longer done. Why? Because so few white people are willing to give their honest opinion on a topic if it would mean disagreeing with a black person. They might believe that a solar powered umbrella is a crazy idea, and that nobody will buy one, but if a black person says they think it's a great idea, they'll agree with him. Just so they won't be accused of hidden "racism" and "prejudice," etc.

So the Bradley Effect should be no surprise to anyone; if anything, we should be shocked that any white person in America is brave enough to admit to a pollster that they plan to vote against a black candidate. In the eyes of the media, black people are good, and white people are bad, so there's really never an excuse for voting for a white candidate if a black guy is in the race. Once again though, just as we did with Eric Holder's "nation of cowards" speech, when it comes to "racism" and voting for or against a black candidate for political office, many conservative whites are missing the bigger point. In fact, we're really dropping the ball on this one, folks.

How? By accepting the media's premise that it would be "racist" to let a candidate's race factor into your choice of who to vote for. When conservatives start talking about this issue, they're always quick to declare, quite vociferously (and on the Internet, often in ALL CAPS with lots of exclamation points!!!!) that race had absolutely nothing to do with how they voted, or that it plays zero part in deciding which candidate to get behind in an upcoming election.

Wrong answer.

The fact that millions of white people think it's somehow immoral or "racist" to prefer to vote for a dogcatcher, governor, member of Congress or president who shares their racial background shows just how incredibly brainwashed almost all of us have become. When you consider that many of these folks would even use terms like "hateful" and "despicable" to describe a white person who would consider race as a factor when voting, you can see just how deeply this message from the media has been implanted in our minds.

Do you think blacks have any compunctions about voting for someone based in part on their skin color? If so, you are not only very naive, but grossly mistaken to boot. Judging from election results in all areas of the country, and going back for several decades, race appears to be one of the primary factors black people consider when deciding which candidate to vote for. According to most reports, Obama received between 95 and 98 percent of all votes cast by blacks in the 2008 election.

Ever heard the media, or any liberals at all, criticize black people for using race as a factor when voting? No, and you never will. The only people you'll ever hear do it are misguided conservatives who think liberals and blacks really mean all this colorblind nonsense they're always spouting, but somehow can't see that they're failing to live up to their own ideals. Yeah, right. And conservatives wonder why we keep losing? No, blacks and liberals don't really believe it's wrong in general to prefer voting for someone of your own race. They only believe it's wrong for a white person to do it. Because that's racism!

Why? Because a racist is a white person!

CHAPTER 9

Barack Obama and the
Magic Negro Dialect

Few things illustrate the hypocrisy of political correctness on race than the "controversy" that erupted in early 2009 over Senator Harry Reid's remarks about Barack Obama. To refresh your memory, a book came out called *Game Change*. It's a book about the presidential campaign of 2008 written by two journalists from *Time* and *New York* magazines. Consisting of a lot of inside baseball and background scenes that the public is never allowed to hear during the campaign itself, the book became a best seller almost overnight.

One of the juicier tidbits was about Senate Majority Leader Harry Reid, one of the top Democrats in the country. It seems he was very impressed with his Senate colleague Barack Obama, and took him aside to encourage him to run for president. This is how the book puts it:

"He [Reid] was wowed by Obama's oratorical gifts and believed that the country was ready to embrace a black presidential candidate, especially one such as Obama — a 'light-skinned' African American 'with no Negro dialect, unless he wanted to have one'..."[36]

Naturally, when this news came out, there was an immediate uproar. The story was the banner headline item on the Drudge Report website for over a day, and it was featured prominently near the top for several days after that. FOX News ran with the story, as did most conservative blogs and websites. The head of the Republican National Committee (RNC), Michael Steele, called for Harry Reid to resign his position as Senate Majority Leader. Several prominent GOP politicians joined the chorus calling for Reid's resignation, including Sen. John Cornyn from Texas, and Sen. Jon Kyl from Arizona. Sarah Palin went on the Bill O'Reilly show and called Reid's comments unacceptable.

The uproar was only coming from white conservatives, though. (Michael Steele doesn't count — he's a token black hired by white conservatives who are ashamed that they're white, in the vain hope that by electing a black man to head up the party, they could convince liberals to stop calling them racists.) On the liberal end of the spectrum, the reaction was quite a bit different.

In fact, beyond "ho-hum," there wasn't much of a reaction from the liberal side. Almost before the ink dried on the book, Reid issued a groveling apology. He also called Barack Obama to personally apologize. Obama, of course, being the big-hearted, selfless saint that he is, forgave him. So did Al Sharpton, and just about every other Democrat, no matter their race, creed or color. (Or sexual orientation!) To them, it was much ado about nothing. Oh, sure, Reid's phrasing was unfortunate, but it's no big deal. Certainly nothing to get all bent out of shape about. Conservatives and Republicans went ballistic, calling the liberals blatant hypocrites for their lack of outrage.

And they certainly had a point. In early 2007, the *Los Angeles Times* printed a column by a writer named David Ehrenstein entitled Obama the Magic Negro. The phrase "magical Negro" is a term used by film buffs to describe the overused movie trope

---

[36]http://www.cnn.com/2010/POLITICS/01/09/obama.reid/index.html

of the wise, compassionate, non-threatening black character who guides or advises or saves the white lead characters, sometimes sacrificing himself in the process. Think *"Driving Miss Daisy."* (Or pretty much any movie with Morgan Freeman in it.) Think *"The Legend of Bagger Vance."* You've seen it a million times if you watch any TV or movies at all.

Did you ever notice that almost any time God is depicted in a movie, the part is played by a black person? (Again, usually Morgan Freeman.) There's a reason for that. Actually, there's a whole bunch of reasons for that, but I'd like to keep this book under a thousand pages...anyway, the magical Negro is a stock character in motion pictures, and blacks often complain that these positive portraits are patronizing and offensive. (Blacks pretty much always complain no matter what you do!) They say these characters aren't "real" or "authentic" black people, but merely fantasies white people like to watch on screen to make themselves feel non-racist. According to this theory, white people absolve themselves of "racism" by thinking that if all black folks were like the wise, benevolent and gentle "magical Negroes" you see in movies, they wouldn't mind a few of them living in their neighborhood as long as they didn't want to date their daughters, etc., etc.

So the column by Ehrenstein on Obama the Magic Negro was basically saying that Barack Obama is functioning as the magical Negro for white voters. In fact, Ehrenstein said that Obama was not only running for president, he was also running to be America's magic Negro, and that the only reason he was so popular with white potential voters was that he wasn't a "real" black man in their eyes. He wasn't "authentic" like Jesse Jackson and Al Sharpton, and so whites weren't too scared or too repelled to vote for him.

The column appeared on March 19, 2007.[37] Thousands—if not tens of thousands—of people read it in the paper or online, including plenty of people in the media, because the *Los Angeles Times* is considered an "important" newspaper. Many liberal

---

[37]http://www.latimes.com/news/opinion/commentary/la-oe-ehrenstein19mar19,0,3391015.story

websites linked to the article, and it wasn't because they thought it was offensive. Liberals and race hustlers had no problem with the column. In fact, they were quite pleased with it, because it was yet another media hit piece on white people who are too "racist" to vote for a real black man, but will vote for Obama because they think of him as not authentically black.

But a couple of days later Rush Limbaugh played a song parody based on the article and all hell broke loose. Set to the tune of *"Puff The Magic Dragon," "Barack, The Magic Negro"* was a hilarious send up of the liberal media and race hustlers. Contrary to what most people think, the song wasn't making fun of Obama at all, but was ridiculing Al Sharpton (and Ehrenstein, the *Los Angeles Times*, and liberals). The singer was even impersonating Sharpton. In the parody, "Sharpton" quoted the article and lamented that an "authentic" black man like himself or Louis Farrakhan can't get white votes; only phony black men like Obama have a chance. In other words, Rush Limbaugh was using brilliant satire to say the exact same thing as Ehrenstein said.

But for the liberals, Rush had gone way too far! They went ballistic, denouncing him (yet again) as a racist, and calling for his head. I won't bother to document their rage in the footnotes — if you somehow missed it, just go to your favorite search engine and put in "Rush Limbaugh magic Negro," and you can spend the rest of the day reading about what a horrible racist Rush Limbaugh is for playing that bit of satire. Knock yourself out!

And while you're at it, do a search for "Chip Saltsman magic Negro" and check out a few of the thousands of pages that turn up. Because in late 2008, a man named Chip Saltsman was running for the job of Republican National Chairman. (It's a shame he didn't win; he would've been far better than Michael Steele. Heck, anybody would be better than Michael Steele!) It turns out that Saltsman is friends with Paul Shanklin, the guy who wrote and performed the parody for Rush Limbaugh. Shanklin has done a bunch of these parodies for the Limbaugh show over the years, and in an effort to drum up votes, Chip Saltsman sent out a CD with about forty of Shanklin's songs to the movers and shakers of the Republican Party who would be voting on who got the vacant Republican National Committee chairman's job. One of the songs was *Barack The Magic Negro*, and once again, all hell broke loose.[38] This time, though, it wasn't just liberals raising Cain. Many Republicans, terrified of being called "racist" and desperate to attract black voters, also condemned Saltsman. (And guess who one of his biggest critics was? Good ol' Michael Steele, that's who. Steele first said the CD wasn't a problem, but at the big candidate showcase before the vote, when there were a lot media present, he opportunistically changed his tune and condemned Saltsman.[39])

Why was it okay for David Ehrenstein to talk about Barack Obama being a magic Negro, but it was wicked "racism" for Rush Limbaugh and Chip Saltsman to talk about it? It's very simple. Ehrenstein is a black man; he can say what he wants and never have to worry about being called a racist. On top of that, his real point was that white people are "racists," and nothing is out of bounds when you're condemning white people for "racism." Limbaugh's parody was "racist" because Rush Limbaugh is a white conservative. He could sing the praises of black people all day long on his radio program, and he would still be a "racist," because he's a white conservative. He only added to his sin by making fun of Al Sharpton and the media.

Which brings us back to Harry Reid and his remarks about Obama being able to attract white votes because he's light skinned and doesn't have a "Negro dialect." He was saying the exact same thing Rush Limbaugh was saying in "*Barack the Magic Negro*," which was based on a column by a black man. But Harry Reid is not a racist. Because he's a liberal, and he was encouraging a black man to run for president, so anything goes. Reid could be caught on tape calling his chauffeur the N-word, and liberals and race hustlers would find a way to excuse him for it. *Because he's a liberal.*

---

[38] http://articles.latimes.com/2008/dec/31/opinion/oe-rutten31
[39] http://thinkprogress.org/2009/01/05/steele-saltsman/

Of course, as I've said repeatedly, liberals are simply deluding themselves if they think that blacks don't think they're "racist." Blacks see them as useful idiots, and even though they believe that all white people are "racists," they give liberals a pass. Liberals don't understand that their certified "non-racist" status is only temporary, and is subject to being revoked at any second if they ever step out of line.

All white people are "racists." Even liberals. They're simply too darned dumb to understand this basic fact.

But what about conservatives? Did they handle the Harry Reid/Negro "scandal" any better? No, they most certainly didn't. Even as I write this, Republicans are still denouncing Reid for his "Negro dialect" remark, which means one thing – they still haven't got a clue.

As usual when it comes to race, Republicans and "conservatives" are doing the exact opposite of what they should be doing. Why are they denouncing Reid for using a perfectly good word? What's wrong with "Negro," anyway? When and why did it suddenly become a bad word? There is nothing offensive in the least about the word Negro, and here's well-known black writer Stanley Crouch saying he's proud to be known as a Negro.[40] Here's another black intellectual, John McWhorter, saying there's nothing wrong with the word.[41] And conservatives should be the last people trying to add yet another word to the list of words white people are not allowed to say. But, as usual, they make complete fools of themselves trying to out-PC the liberals and Democrats, and pandering to blacks on this "controversy."

Sarah Palin called the word "unacceptable" on the Bill O'Reilly show.[42] She never said, why it's unacceptable of course, (because she can't, because it's not) and she would be the first one to boast about supporting the United Negro College Fund and praise it to the skies if the topic ever came up. But Palin looks like a genius compared to the black "conservatives" out there.

[40]http://www.nydailynews.com/opinions/2010/01/11/2010-01-11_then__now_im_a_negro.html
[41]http://video.nytimes.com/video/2010/01/15/opinion/1247466575260/bloggingheads-in-defense-of-negro.html
[42]http://blog.vdare.com/archives/2010/01/13/its-about-time-sara-palin-said-something-interesting-how-about-immigration-moratorium/

Frankly, conservatives really blew it with the "Negro dialect" uproar, especially by letting black "conservatives" spout off about how "hateful" Reid's remark was. If you doubt me, look up some quotes from these black "conservatives" on the Harry Reid/Negro dialect "scandal." Here's one from WorldNetDaily columnist Mychal Massie:

> "Reid is a loathsome individual whose apology was based on exposure not repentance. Reid's comments are proof positive that the racial animus of the past is alive and prevalent among liberals today..."[43]

Really? Using the word *Negro* to describe a Negro now makes a person "loathsome?" So loathsome and filled with "animus" that he stands in need of repentance?

Good Lord? These are the people who are supposed to be on our side? This is conservatism?

Two of the two best-known up and coming black Republicans are Lloyd Marcus and Allan West. White conservative Tea Party types swoon over everything they say, and they're promoting these two so much that, to a lot of people, the Tea Party movement looks more like the Uncle Tom Party movement. Blacks are about .0000001 percent of the people who make up the Tea Party movement, and show up at the rallies, but somehow these two black men have become the public faces of the Tea Party movement.[44] Lloyd Marcus said Reid "insulted" him,[45] and Allen West posted a completely unhinged rant about Reid, slavery and the KKK,[46] and demanded that Reid resign.

Resign? For saying *Negro*?

And he's a black "conservative?" I'd hate to hear what black liberals think about what words white people shouldn't use. But the other sixteen black "conservatives" in America seem to agree with West that saying Negro is a wicked, vile sin.

---

[43]http://www.nationalcenter.org/2010/01/project-21-members-comment-on-harry.html
[44]http://www.amren.com/mtnews/archives/2010/01/black_conservat_1.php
[45]http://www.resistnet.com/profiles/blogs/lloyd-marcus-the-clue-missed?xg_source=activity
[46]http://ow.ly/V862

This is one of the main reasons why many conservative groups and movements go nowhere. In a futile attempt to pander to blacks and get the media to stop calling them "racists," they elevate just about any black person that shows up to a position of prominence. As soon as they come on board, the white leadership starts promoting them in the vain hopes the movement won't get called racist, which never works. Then the black "conservatives" start talking about how the Democrats are the real racists who want to keep blacks on the liberal plantation, etc., etc., etc., and before you know it, the whole movement has been derailed, and the focus turns to how the other guys are more racist than we are, and we're better for blacks than the liberals are, etc.

Suddenly, what was supposed to be a revolt against big government turns into one lecture after another about racism, except this time it's the Democrats who are the bad guys, and not the Republicans. Why a movement that's 99 percent white should be so all-fired concerned about what blacks want is never explained, even as it becomes one of the primary talking points. And lots of would-be supporters shake their heads in disgust and never get on board, while a lot of followers quit for the same reason. If they want to hear about "racism" and what's good for blacks all the time, they can watch MSNBC. And the movement eventually fizzles out, just as the Tea Party movement will.

Instead of getting anything done, these movements that promote people like Marcus and West simply because they're black make themselves look like idiots. They don't attract blacks with their nonsense, they disgust their white supporters, and in the end they destroy themselves. But at least they can brag about how non-racist they are as America goes down the tubes.

What really took the cake though, was Republicans denouncing Democrats as having a "double standard" because they didn't give Harry Reid the same treatment Trent Lott got back in 2002. Lott, you might remember, was the GOP Senator from Mississippi and Senate Majority Leader who caught all kinds of hell for being nice to a 100-year-old man. He told Strom Thurmond at his 100th birthday party that if America had voted for him when he ran for president, we wouldn't' have had near as many problems as we've had.

Which was 100 percent true; but that's beside the point. Trent Lott was humoring a man on his hundredth birthday. No one takes anything said to a 100-year-old man on his birthday seriously. What Lott said was the equivalent of telling him that he didn't look a day over forty. He was just being nice to a really old man on his special day.

Nevertheless, Trent Lott was widely condemned for his remarks, and pressured to step down from his position as Senate Majority Leader. His words were described as "disgraceful," "indefensible," "appalling" and "shameful," among other denunciations. One man went even further, calling them "insensitive," "inexcusable," and even "repugnant" on national TV. So, yes, it certainly does look like Democrats have a double standard when it comes to race.

Except that the quotes in the paragraph above are from Republicans, not Democrats.[47] Yes, Democrats did condemn Lott for his remarks, but it was a few Republican pundits who first started raising hell about the remarks in the media. David Frum, Charles Krauthammer, Jonah Goldberg and William Kristol aren't Democrats; they're well known Republicans. And they're the ones who started beating the drums for Trent Lott to resign as Senate Majority Leader. And the man who went on national television and denounced the remarks as "insensitive," "inexcusable, " and "repugnant?" That was a Republican, too. Those remarks were made by *Trent Lott himself* in an interview on the BET network. In the same interview he also denounced Mississippi as a "wicked" state, apologized for voting against the MLK holiday, and raved about how much he loves affirmative action and would like to see even more of it.[48] And Democrats didn't force Trent Lott to resign as Senate Majority Leader; Republicans did. Republicans voted Lott into that office. Democrats have no say in internal GOP matters.

---

[47]http://vdare.com/francis/lott2.htm
[48]http://archives.cnn.com/2002/ALLPOLITICS/12/16/lott.controversy/index.html

Lott should have resigned. Not for his remarks to Strom Thurmond, which were fine, but for his disgusting display of groveling after the uproar began, which was itself started by Republicans. What kind of a man goes on national TV and calls his state a "wicked" place? This sniveling traitor should have been booted out of his office, and then tarred and feathered when he got back home. And the Republican Party should be ashamed of itself for condemning his remarks at a birthday party for a 100-year-old man. But they're not. To this day, the GOP is proud of what they did to Trent Lott. When it comes to race, the people who run the Republican Party will always try to outdo the Democrats when it comes to groveling and pandering to non-whites, and enforcing Political Correctness.

Why? Because their supporters are white, and all white people are racists. That's not something that just liberals and non-whites believe. The Republican Party believes it too, and they're ashamed that they're a party of "racists," so they're always trying to find a way to condemn their own supporters in a bid to win favor with non-whites and the media. It never works, but they never stop trying. But why do white people keep supporting a party that hates them? That's the real mystery.

CHAPTER 10

There's a Pot of Black Republicans at the End of the Rainbow

Republican politicians and conservative commentators love to tell us (over and over and over and over...) that, deep down, black people are really conservatives, and one of these days they're going to start voting en masse for conservative Republican candidates. You even hear this nonsense from people like Rush Limbaugh and Sean Hannity, and even (gasp!) Ann Coulter. Yes, right now black people vote Democrat by margins of 9 to 1 or higher, but that's all going to change any day now, and when it does, that sweet chariot will finally swing low and carry us all to the promised land of a permanent Republican majority!

That's the theory, anyway... And I must admit, as theories go, it's real nice. It really tugs at the heartstrings. Just think of it: one day soon all God's children will hold hands and march to the polling place in one accord and pull that GOP lever, and America will suffer no more from those evil liberals. Once blacks see the light and come together with conservative white folks to give us a Republican Congress and a Republican president, we'll finally be able to enact a conservative agenda. There will be no more big-spending federal government, no more abortion, no more racial quotas, no more minority set-asides, no more condemnations of "racial profiling," no more welfare programs, etc.

(You know — just like when we had a Republican president and Congress from 2001 to 2007!)

Unfortunately, this great day when Kingdom Come finally comes, not only will never get here, it never even seems to get any closer. Like a mirage in the desert, it's always just out of reach. It always seems to be just around the corner, just down the road, gonna happen any day now, etc. The GOP politicians and conservative pundits keep assuring us that we're right on the verge of this incredible breakthrough, and when it happens, look out brother, because that'll be all she wrote for liberalism in this country!

Hallelujah!

Praise the Lord!

Free at last! Free at last!

Oops, sorry...I got so caught up in reading some of this rainbow conservative stuff I thought the day had actually arrived. But no, it's still not here. But like I said, it's a real nice theory; heck, you can get teary-eyed just thinking about it. Just imagine: Nancy Pelosi would be back home spending time with her grandchildren. Barney Frank and his "husband" could finally make time for Barney's speech therapy sessions. Maxine Waters would be asking people if they want fries with their burger. Al Sharpton and Jesse Jackson would be in prison for fraud, and Barack Obama would have to go back to "organizing the community" in order to make a living. Of course, since "the community" would now be solidly Republican, he'd probably be forced to move in with his good buddy William Ayers, the former terrorist. Yeah, it would sure be nice if black people started voting for conservatives.

But if I were you, I wouldn't waste any time thinking it's

actually going to happen. In fact, I can assure you that it's never going to happen. That's right; black people are never going to vote in any appreciable numbers for candidates who promise smaller government. Black people *like* big government. They don't want to see a roll-back of welfare, or racial quotas, or affirmative action, or fewer "civil rights" or "hate crimes" bills. Why would they? These programs are massive benefit packages for them that come mainly at the expense of white people. They would be crazy to want to reverse liberalism.

I mean, think about it...if millions of white people moved to Nigeria for some unfathomable reason, and the government of Nigeria began establishing quotas and other policies to force black business owners to hire white people, and began giving out massive welfare subsidies that whites received far out of proportion to their percentage of the population, and passed law after law requiring Nigerian blacks to treat white people as privileged citizens who must never be criticized or insulted, and started turning every altercation between a white and a black into an "anti-white hate crime" while downplaying every white-on-black crime no matter how violent...well, how many white people in Nigeria would vote to change things? *Not very many.* So why would blacks in America react any differently?

Expecting large numbers of black people to start voting for conservatives because they want a smaller government, is about like expecting the American Association of Retired Persons to start demanding that Social Security be abolished, or the AFL-CIO to start endorsing candidates who promise to repeal minimum wage laws. Can you imagine the National Football League agitating to restore obsolete laws against playing sports on Sunday, or Bill Clinton demanding that adultery be outlawed? Of course not. But those scenarios are about as likely to happen as blacks voting for conservatives in large numbers. Any conservative who thinks that one of these days millions of black people are going to suddenly turn into Ronald Reagan with an Afro and a tan is crazy enough to be certified as an MSNBC talk show host.

Unfortunately, many conservatives (and almost all conservative leaders) prefer living in a fantasy world rather than dealing with cold, hard reality. They seem to believe that if Republicans just close their eyes and squeeze real hard, and click their heels together, and proclaim "Martin Luther King, Jr. was a Republican!" enough times, and elevate enough unqualified tokens like Michael Steele to leadership positions, their fantasy will come true. What's even worse is that the more blacks ignore the GOP, the more the GOP bends over backwards to pander and grovel to them. They continually screw over white people, their only supporters, in order to curry favor with a group that votes 9 to 1 against them.

Then they wonder why they keep losing elections! Gee, I dunno. That's a real head-scratcher there. You think it might have something to do with constantly stabbing your supporters in the back while sucking up to people who hate your guts and will never vote for you? Call me crazy, but that might be something worth looking into, Republicans. The general operating theory of politics is that when you gain power you reward your supporters, and punish those who oppose you. But the Republicans won't do that, because their supporters are conservative white people, and, as everyone knows, conservative white people are racists. So they do the opposite. They constantly betray their base of white voters, while endlessly pandering to blacks. Yeah, that's a recipe for electoral victory!

There's a name for conservatives who think this way: "rainbow conservatives." They really believe (or at least claim they really believe) that deep down, people are people — black people are exactly the same as white people who are exactly the same as Asians who are exactly the same as Hispanics who are exactly the same as blacks, etc. There may be a few cultural differences, but they're trivial, and basically we're all the same. Their favorite saying is "there's only one race — the human race!" Yeah, I know, it's hard to believe otherwise intelligent people could fall for such nonsense, but millions of conservatives do. Or at least pretend to. A whole bunch of them are just spouting this foolishness because they don't want to be accused of "racism." But there is definitely a large segment of conservatives who actually believe this tripe.

If you have a friend who is one of those conservatives who believe that one of these days black people are going to start voting for conservative candidates, you should ask him a few simple questions. For starters, if all these black people are really all that conservative deep down in their hearts, then why aren't they voting Republican now? What are they waiting for? If your friend is like most rainbow conservatives, he'll try to explain that by saying that blacks don't understand that the Democrats are just using them for their votes, and that their liberal policies are destroying the black community. Or he'll say that blacks need to stop listening to their leaders like Jesse Jackson and Al Sharpton and start thinking for themselves.

In other words, rainbow conservatives believe that most black people are incredibly stupid. They're unable to think for themselves; they're just helpless overgrown children who can't figure out what's in their own best interests, so they listen to paternal figures like Jesse and Al, Barney Frank and Nancy Pelosi. It's our job as conservatives to get it through black people's incredibly thick skulls that doing what liberals and "civil rights" leaders tell them to do is bad for them, and instead, they should start voting for the candidates white conservatives tell them to vote for. They won't put it quite this bluntly, of course; you'll rarely hear one of them actually come out and say that blacks vote for Democrats because they're too stupid to understand their own interests, even though that's exactly what they're saying when you break it down.

Instead, you'll hear conservative pundits and politicians talk about Democrats "keeping blacks on the liberal plantation," etc.[49] Just think about that for a minute, and let the incredible condescension and flat out paternalism sink in. Black people in America are on a plantation? And they're being kept there

---

[49]http://www.google.com/search?rlz=1C1GGLS_enUS291US337&sourceid=chrome&ie=UTF-8&q=blacks+"liberal+plantation"

against their will by liberals and race-hustling preachers? And they're too stupid to even realize it? Honestly, that's about as offensive as you can get when talking about a group of adult voters with free will, and yet you hear this kind of talk from conservatives all the time.

And just how are liberals pulling off this incredible feat? In America, we vote in secret; no one can tell us who we have to vote for, or watch us to make sure we vote the "right" way. Yet somehow liberals are sneaking into these private voting booths and making black people vote Democrat? No, of course not. The ninety percent of black people who vote Democrat do it because they want to. They choose to, of their own free will, because they believe voting for liberals is in their best interests. No one is forcing them to do anything; let alone "keeping them on the liberal plantation" against their will.

Rainbow conservatives can't accept this indisputable fact, because it flies in the face of everything they believe about race. If we're all equal, and people are pretty much the same across the board, then voting patterns should be pretty similar across racial lines. But they're not. White people are the only ones who split their votes between the parties in any meaningful way. The other races heavily favor the Democrats. Blacks vote about 9-1 Democrat, and Hispanics vote about 2-1 Democrat. They've been doing so for a long, long time, and there is absolutely no reason to believe they're going to change. The best predictor of future behavior is past behavior.[50]

This inconvenient fact makes a mockery of the idea that people are pretty much all the same and there's no such thing as racial differences. Since that's one of the core beliefs of rainbow conservatives, they have to come up with some way to account for their theory not working. So they make up a ludicrous theory that liberals and black preachers are somehow "forcing" or "tricking" black people into voting for liberalism. It never seems to dawn on them that this assumes black voters are so stupid that

---

[50]And please don't tell me I'm wrong about racial voting patterns not changing by pointing to the fact that the Republican Party used to win the black vote. Yes, they did. That's because back then, the GOP was more liberal than the Democrats. The racial voting pattern didn't change at all; the black (and Hispanic) vote has always gone to the more liberal of the two parties.

they're incapable of analyzing ballot issues and forming their own opinions, and are just led down the primrose path by those fast talking liberals. Yeah, that's a real winner, Republicans. Lots of luck with that permanent GOP majority thing!

And where on earth did this idea come from that most blacks are "conservatives on social issues" and "family values" are important to them? That has got to be just about the most idiotic notion I've ever heard. It isn't just wrong; it's the exact opposite of the truth. But countless Republicans and conservatives have so little self-respect that they'll actually make that statement in public. And they'll do it over and over again. They would rather make complete jackasses of themselves than admit that there are important differences between the races, and nowhere are these differences as stark as when it comes to "social issues."

Family values are a huge priority with black people? Yeah, right. Rainbow conservatives love to point to the Proposition 8 vote in California in 2008 as "proof" that black voters are conservative on traditional moral values. Proposition 8, of course, was the ballot initiative to repeal legalized same-sex marriage in the Golden State. It passed by a margin of about four points. According to exit polls, 49 percent of whites voted to repeal gay marriage, while 70 percent of blacks did. The rainbow conservatives were ecstatic. This was the sign that the dam was breaking, and that the saints were about to come marching in! Black voters had finally started to "get it," and they weren't gonna work on ol' Massa Libr'l's plantation no mo'! They'll put up with a lot, but when those dang old liberals started messing with marriage, black voters put their foot down and said enough is enough.

"Gosh darn it," gushed the rainbow conservatives, "traditional marriage is something blacks care very deeply about." Really? Then why don't a few of them try getting married for themselves? Why are nearly three out of 4 of their children born out of wedlock?[51] The rate is steadily increasing; in 2007 it was 72 percent, and by now it's got to be pushing 75

---

[51]http://www.amren.com/mtnews/archives/2009/04/out-of-wedlock.php

percent, if it hasn't passed that figure. That's nearly three times the white rate, by the way. And in many of the white cases, the parents actually go on to get married and form a family. That's a lot less likely when the parents are black. Most black children grow up in homes headed by unmarried women.[52] If that's not shocking enough to dissuade rainbow conservatives from the lunatic idea that "family values" are important to most blacks, how about this — more and more black people say they don't know anyone who is married![53] Think about that for a minute. Imagine not knowing anyone who's married. Actually, I doubt if you can imagine such a thing. For white people, that's pretty much inconceivable. For blacks, it's becoming more and more common. So, please, rainbow conservatives, spare us any more talk about the importance of traditional marriage to most black people.

Abortion? Black women abort their babies at nearly five times the rate of white women, according to the *Washington Post*, quoting the Guttmacher Institute.[54] And "family values" are important to blacks? Whatever. And just think of what the illegitimacy rate would be among blacks if their rate of abortion weren't so high... And how about kids in foster care? Black kids wind up in foster care at about six times the rate of white kids.[55] Is that because strong families are a priority with black people? And if blacks are so conservative on social issues, why is it so many of them choose a life of crime? Blacks are seven to eight times more likely to commit crimes than white people.[56]

I could go on and on, but I'm not going to. It's outrageous that I even had to bring up these facts. Having to demonstrate that "social issues" and "family values" aren't high priorities with most blacks is about like having to prove that midgets rarely make the NBA All Star team. It's not even an arguable issue. Debate over. Case closed. Unless you're a rainbow conservative

---

[52]http://datacenter.kidscount.org/data/acrossstates/Rankings.aspx?ind=107

[53]http://www.boston.com/yourlife/relationships/articles/2006/08/09/younger_blacks_absorb_a_wariness_of_marriage/

[54]http://www.washingtonpost.com/wp-dyn/content/article/2008/09/22/AR2008092202831.html

[55]http://www.adopting.org/adoptions/learn-about-adoption-waiting-children.html

[56]http://www.colorofcrime.com/colorofcrime2005.html

who prefers living in La La Land to dealing with reality. They'll claim to believe anything, no matter how ludicrous, if they think it might stop people from calling them racists. Of course, they just get called racists anyway, but they never learn.

Rainbow conservatives would be merely pathetic if there were only a few of them. Unfortunately, there are millions of them, and they are now in charge of the Republican Party. There is only one racial group in America that votes Republican in any substantial numbers—white people. But the people who run the GOP are convinced that they can change that. So they go out of their way to attract non-whites, and to constantly insult, ignore and betray whites. They do this for two reasons. The first is that they take us for granted. Conservative white folks are never going to vote for Democrats, so they think they have nothing to worry about, and are free to abuse us however they see fit, confident that we'll put up with it because we have no other alternatives.

But they're wrong. It might be the case that there aren't any other parties to vote for if you're a white conservative, but that doesn't mean you have to vote Republican. You have another choice — stay home on election day and don't vote for anybody. In 2008 millions of white people did just that, after being disgusted by John McCain's constant pandering and groveling to non-whites. This "strategy" also turns off a lot of moderate white voters, who may not be all that conservative on some issues, but increasingly see that GOP as just a "me-too" version of the Democratic Party and it's focus on non-white interests.

What's the second reason the GOP is hell-bent on committing suicide by ignoring its base and pandering to non-whites, who are never going to vote for them? Well, you can probably guess. Yep, it's because they don't want to be called "racists" for standing up for white interests, and treating white voters as people worthy of respect, and not just a bunch of hate-filled racists like the media portrays us. They demonize any candidate who would dare utter so much as a peep about sticking up for the interests of white people.

The leadership of the Republican Party knows what the media would do to them if they started being frank about race. That's why they'll never admit that non-whites are always going to vote for the more liberal party, and that trying to attract their votes is a complete waste of time, and they should actually focus on getting out the white vote.

They'd rather destroy themselves than be called "racists" by the media, which is about as stupid as it gets. Because, as we've seen time and time again in this book and in the daily headlines, it doesn't matter what the GOP does, or how obsequious and apologetic they are to non-whites. No matter how much they suck up, they still get called "racists" by the media. Just ask John McCain.

Chapter 11

Trinity United Church of Hate

If there is one thing that really demonstrates the hypocrisy about "racism" in America beyond the shadow of any doubt, it's the Jeremiah Wright story from the 2008 presidential election. I'm sorry; make that "Reverend" Jeremiah Wright. ("Reverend" is apparently an old Swahili word for "I hate honkies." As in Rev. Jesse Jackson, Rev. Al Sharpton, Rev. Martin Luther King, Jr., etc, etc.) In any sane country, Jeremiah Wright would have been the kiss of death for any political candidate who had been a member of his church for nearly twenty years.

If America hadn't gone insane in the past fifty years on the issue of "racism," Barack Hussein Obama would never be electable as dog-catcher, let alone President of the United States. Yet, Jeremiah Wright's unabashed hatred of white people not only didn't prove to be any hurdle to the White House for Obama, by now most people have forgotten all about it. You can thank the media for that (and John McCain deserves a big tip of the hat, too).

For most Americans, the first clue they had that something was amiss at Obama's "church" was when ABC broadcast several video snippets from some of Wright's sermons. I'm sure we all remember the "God bless America? Naw, naw, naw — God damn America!" and "the US of KKKA" quotes. But these came as no surprise to any conservative who's politically aware, because this stuff had been all over the Internet for months before the national media dared touch the story.[57] In fact, it's almost certainly the case that the only reason the media finally reported the story was because right-wingers had been talking about this stuff for so long that word was finally beginning to filter out to millions of people, and the media knew they couldn't ignore it much longer without making their pro-Obama bias even clearer.

So, eventually it came out, and millions of Americans were stunned to learn that Barack Obama, the Democratic nominee for president, who had branded himself as the "post-racial" candidate and, because of his biracial background, was perfectly poised to bring the races of America together, had spent nearly twenty years listening to this goon spew this kind of outright hatred of white people every Sunday. And he was The One who was going to "heal" America of "racism" by getting elected to the White House? Understandably, Middle America was quite shocked to discover that Obama wasn't the person they thought he was at all.

And the brief video snippets of Wright's ranting and raving about evil honky America were just the tip of the iceberg. Wright's Chicago church, Trinity United Church of Christ (TUCC), publishes a magazine called *Trumpet*. In 2007, it presented a special award called the Dr. Jeremiah A. Wright, Jr. Lifetime Achievement Trumpeter Award. The honoree was cited as a man who "truly epitomized greatness." Jeremiah Wright described the honoree as "an unforgettable force, a catalyst for change and a religious leader who is sincere about his faith and purpose." Wright

---

[57]http://www.vdare.com/Sailer/070325_obama.htm

went on to call the honoree a man of "integrity and honesty" and praised his "depth of analysis when it comes to the racial ills of this nation."[58] Wow, he sounds like quite a guy. So who was this saint who was deemed worthy of the Lifetime Achievement award named after Jeremiah Wright himself? Why, it was none other than white-hating lunatic Louis Farrakhan.

When this news came out, Obama's handlers tried to downplay the situation, and the media let them get away with it. In fact, the media was pretty much a full partner in the Obama campaign the entire time, and this episode was no exception. We were once again assured that Obama, just like most devout Christians, doesn't always agree with his pastor. Which is true enough, except that most people's disagreements with their pastors are over minor issues, such as the proper translation of a Greek or Hebrew phrase, or what kind of hymns should be sung in the worship service. They're not over questions about whether white people invented AIDS to kill off blacks, or the proper pronunciation of "blue-eyed devils," one of Farrakhan's terms for white people. These aren't mere quibbles; anyone who wouldn't leave a church as soon as these views became known obviously doesn't have a big problem with the views being expressed. A man who sat in the church for nearly twenty years, and named his book after one of Wright's hate-whitey sermons obviously either agrees with Jeremiah Wright, or thinks his reprehensible hate of white people is not anything to get excited about. Furthermore, since from the looks of things (keep reading!) about the only thing preached at Trinity United Church of Christ was hatred of white people, I'd love to know what Obama *agreed* with Wright about. It's not as if these incidents were slips of the tongue. You don't give a hate filled lunatic like Louis Farrakhan a Lifetime Achievement award named after yourself by accident. And something like that doesn't come out of left field. Besides, Wright and Farrakhan have been close pals for years; Wright even accompanied Farrakhan on a trip to the Middle East way back in 1984.

---

[58] http://www.washingtonpost.com/wp-dyn/content/article/2008/01/14/AR2008011402083.html

So the "few minor disagreements" argument won't fly. They weren't minor by any stretch of the imagination, and they certainly weren't few. I might have exaggerated a minute ago when I said that it looks like hatred of white people was pretty much the only thing being preached at Trinity United Church of Christ, but it wasn't much of an exaggeration. Black hatred of white people was one of the defining themes of the church, and there is no way Obama could have missed that. Nobody could have missed it, in fact, even if they were just driving past TUCC. Like many churches, Trinity United has stained glass windows. Trinity United Church of Christ's stained glass work is quite a bit different most churches, however, whose stained glass windows feature scenes from the Bible, or great Christian saints. Guess who's on TUCC's windows? Well, Martin Luther King, Jr. for one; hardly a saint by anyone's definition. He was a plagiarist and a notorious adulterer. But it gets worse — their stained glass window also features Malcolm X![59]

What kind of Christian church would have a stained glass image of Malcolm X in their window? That tells you all you need to know about what Trinity United Church of Christ is all about. It's certainly not about any kind of Christianity an evangelical Christian would recognize. Malcolm X despised Christianity. He called it the white man's religion, and vigorously denounced it. He was a Black Muslim, a member of the Nation of Islam, which is the kooky race hate cult now presided over by Jeremiah Wright Lifetime Achievement honoree Louis Farrakhan. To put it bluntly, Malcolm X hated everything Christianity stood for. No Christian church would even consider honoring him with a stained glass window in a building supposedly dedicated to the teachings of Jesus Christ. Any "church" that would think he deserves any kind of honor isn't a Christian institution. But that doesn't matter. Malcolm X may have hated Christianity, but he also hated the white man. That's why TUCC feels like he deserves to have a stained glass window in his honor. And Barack Hussein Obama attended this church for nearly twenty

---

[59]http://www.time.com/time/nation/article/0,8599,1724976,00.html

years and it never bothered him that they would honor a man who not only hated white people, but also hated the Christian religion? And he promised to be the "post-racial" president?

And we've still only scratched the surface of the racial hate that is the foundation of Trinity United Church of Christ. If you go to their website, you can see for yourself that it's not a Christian church by any stretch of the imagination; it's a black race cult that teaches hatred of white people. It's just the Nation of Islam under a different name, which attracts black people who want to indulge their hatred of white people while still calling themselves Christians. That's why Jeremiah Wright and Louis Farrakhan are such good pals; they're not practicing separate religions at all. They share the same religion — hatred of the white man.

Go to their website and read the page about their most important principles, called The Black Value System.[60] During the short-lived uproar over Jeremiah Wright the church briefly took this page down. Now that Obama is safely in the White House, they feel free to put it back up for the entire world to see. One glance at it and you'll see why they took it down. Because anyone reading this document would understand immediately that Trinity United Church of Christ isn't a religious organization at all; it's a racial organization using religion as a prop to disguise their hatred.

It's really important that you don't just take my word for this. You really need to go to TUCC's website and check it out for yourself. They make it kind of hard to find — the easiest way is to go to your favorite search engine and type in "black value system;" it should be the first site that comes up. You'll see with your own eyes that at TUCC, where Obama spent twenty years, everything revolves around and is focused on blackness. It's an outrageous lie to claim that Wright's hate filled remarks were just the result of "going too far" or using "intemperate language" on rare occasions as Obama, his handlers and the media have done. I'm not going to reproduce the entire document in this

---

[60]http://www.tucc.org/index.php?option=com_content&task=view&id=114

book. But let's look at some of the main planks of the Black Value System preached at Obama's Trinity United Church of Hate Whitey. One of their first planks is:

The highest level of achievement for any Black person must be a contribution of strength and continuity of the Black Community

Just try to imagine the media reaction if a white candidate belonged to a church that taught that contributing to the White Community was a white person's highest achievement. We all know how that would turn out. They would be hounded until they dropped out of the race in disgrace; they wouldn't get off by just quitting the church as Obama did.

Here's another one:

The Black family circle must generate strength, stability and love, despite the uncertainty of externals, because these characteristics are required if the developing person is to withstand warping by our racist competitive society.

By "competitive," they mean a capitalist as opposed to a socialist economy. Capitalism is one of the ways evil white folks keep the black man down, as Jeremiah Wright has stated over and over. And "racist" society? You know what that means — America is a majority-white country, and white people are evil racists, so American society is hopelessly racist. At TUCC, it's all about loving blacks, and hating whites who are the cause of all black people's problems. And here's a real gem in #8:

Disavowal of the Pursuit of "Middleclassness." Classic methodology on control of captives teaches that captors must be able to identify the "talented tenth" of those subjugated, especially those who show promise of providing the kind of leadership that might threaten the captor's control.

Captives? Captors? Subjugation? That's pretty hard to miss. Black people are "captives" of us evil white folks who use the system to "subjugate" the black man. And we're supposed to believe that "God damn America!" and "the U.S. of KKKA" were just slips of the tongue from Jeremiah Wright? They go on to list a few of the ways the evil white man "subjugates" his black "captives" in America:

Killing them off directly, and/or fostering a social system that encourages them to kill off one another.

Placing them in concentration camps, and/or structuring an economic environment that induces captive youth to fill the jails and prisons.

How much hate do you have to have in your heart to write something like this, or attend a church that believes this for two decades? Or to name your book after a sermon title of the man who preaches this garbage every Sunday? Blacks aren't at fault when they "kill off one another," as they do at extremely high rates in America. No, they're simply victims of a racist system that encourages them to do it. And if the evil white man can't convince enough blacks to kill each other, we have a backup plan — "structuring an economic environment" that "induces" captive black youths to fill our jails and prisons.

Again, try to imagine a white man running for president who belonged to a church that preached that white criminals aren't really bad people; they're simply helpless victims of black people who don't choose a life of crime, but fall into it because black people hate them, render them helpless, and induce them into robbing, raping and murdering people. How many excuses would the mass media make for a man like that? We all know the answer — they would be denouncing him for the next fifty years, and his life in politics would be over. He'd be lucky to be able to get a job at McDonald's.

But when a black candidate belongs to a church that teaches this hateful lunacy about whites, it's no big deal.

Because a non-white person, no matter how filled with hate they are toward whites, can't be a racist. So the media and liberals will invent any excuse, no matter how ludicrous, to rationalize and justify non-white hatred of white people.

Meanwhile, any white person who had ever said anything that was 1/100th as hateful toward blacks as what TUCC preaches on their website about blacks would be the reincarnation of Bull Connor.

Why? Because "racist" means white person.

By now, this should be getting much, much clearer. But if you're still having trouble with the concept, keep reading. Because we haven't plumbed the depths of the burning hatred of white people at the "church" Barack Obama attended for almost two decades. Oh, no — there's still worse. Far worse.

When more and more of this stuff started coming out, and Obama's handlers and the media began panicking, the media spin went into overdrive. First they told us that this stuff was taken out of context. Which is a lie. Go to the website and read the Black Value System for yourself. The Black Value System is the context of TUCC, and it's dripping with black race consciousness and hatred of white people. It's their mission statement, and they spell out it clearly.

Then the media started telling us that Jeremiah Wright was hardly out of the ordinary when it comes to black preachers, and that Trinity United Church of Hate is considered to be a mainstream black church. Black preachers preach with a "prophetic voice," etc., etc., and white people aren't smart enough to "understand" what they're really saying. But there's nothing to be concerned about, because nearly all of them talk this way from the pulpit. Well, that's a relief. White people shouldn't be concerned that Obama's church is built on hatred of whites and preaches it non-stop, because that's what almost all black churches and preachers believe and preach!

(By the way — they're lying when they say it's not really hate, and that black churches and preachers don't really mean this stuff, but they're telling the truth when they say that it's what you'll hear at many, if not most black churches on a typical Sunday. White people have no idea what goes on in black churches, and would be shocked if they found out. Actually, they did find out when Jeremiah Wright hit the fan, but thanks to the liberals and the media they quickly forgot about it. It should have been a wake-up call for white Americans, but it wasn't. Just like the videos of blacks all over America cheering the O.J. Simpson acquittal should have been a wake-up call, but wasn't. We'd better start answering these wake-up calls before it's too late!)

Finally, Obama's apologists in the media patiently explained to us that there was nothing wrong with the kind of undisguised hatred of white people preached by Jeremiah Wright and espoused in TUCC's Black Value System, because it's based on the work of a prominent black theologian.

The theologian is named James Cone. Never heard of him? Most people hadn't; especially white people. (Of course, if he was white, and saying the reverse of what James Cone teaches, we'd never hear the end of him from the media. He'd be the public face of Christianity.) This argument really takes the cake. It's like saying that someone who idolizes Jeffrey Dahmer isn't bad because he's also a big fan of John Wayne Gacy! I'm not exaggerating. Get a load of James Cone for yourself. Here are some quotes from his written works.

"Black theology refuses to accept a God who is not identified totally with the goals of the black community. If God is not for us and against white people, then he is a murderer, and we had better kill him. The task of black theology is to kill Gods who do not belong to the black community ... Black theology will accept only the love of God which [sic] participates in the destruction of the white enemy. What we need is the divine love as expressed in Black Power, which is the power of black people to destroy their oppressors here and now by any means at their disposal. Unless God is participating in this holy activity, we must reject his love."[61]

Nice, huh? Black Christianity has no use for a god who's not out to destroy their enemies, white people. And you thought my Jeffrey Dahmer/John Wayne Gacy comparison was a bit over the top, didn't you? What do you think of it now, white man? And this is the theology on which Obama's Trinity United Church of Christ is based! And Obama nearly spent his entire adult life "worshiping" at this abomination! He reveres the man who preaches this filth, and named his book after one of his anti-white sermons! And if you thought I overstated my case earlier when I said that TUCC wasn't about religion at all, but about race, and that for them their blackness is their religion, check this out:

To be Christian is to be one of those whom God has chosen. God has chosen black people![62]

How much clearer can you get? If you're still somehow in doubt, he makes it even more explicit here:

[L]iberal whites want to be white and Christian at the same time; but they fail to realize that this approach is a contradiction in terms — Christianity and whiteness are opposites.[63]

Get a load of this one:

Theologically, Malcolm X was not far wrong when he called the white man 'the devil.' The white structure of this American society, personified in every racist, must be at least part of what the New Testament meant by the demonic forces.[64]

[61]http://www.wnd.com/index.php?fa=PAGE.view&pageId=59230
[62]http://www.amren.com/mtnews/archives/2008/04/obamas_pastor_s.php
[63]http://www.discoverthenetworks.org/individualProfile.asp?indid=2315
[64]http://www.discoverthenetworks.org/individualProfile.asp?indid=2315

Can you feel the love? I knew that lunatics like James Cone, Jeremiah Wright and Trinity United Church of Hate believe that Jesus was black. I had no idea they thought he was a Black Muslim. And, evidently, "prominent black theologian" is an old Swahili phrase meaning head honky hater in charge.

There you have it, white man. That's what Barack Hussein Obama thinks of you and your family. The god he worships is out to destroy you, and every other white enemy on the face of the earth. That's why Jesus came, to kill the white man. If Jesus wasn't out to kill the white man, blacks wouldn't worship him, because he would be a false god. That's what James Cone says. And Jeremiah Wright considers him to be the person who has influenced his thinking the most. He was so impressed with Cone that he and Trinity United Church of Hate created their Black Value System based on Cone's raging, seething hatred of white people.

And we're expected to believe that in nearly twenty years of church attendance Barack Obama never noticed any of this stuff?

That it never occurred to him to ask someone why a Christian church would have a portrait of a radical Black Muslim who preached violence in its stained glass window?

That Obama was just sort of joking around when he named his book after one of Jeremiah Wright's vicious anti-white sermons?

Yes, liberals and the media do expect us to believe this stuff. And millions of us fell for it, or Obama wouldn't be in the White House today.

And, remember, the man who spent nearly his entire adult life in this Church of Hate Whitey is the same person who had the gall to turn around order his Attorney General to lecture us on the evils of segregated churches.

And don't ever forget these, either:

Barack Obama is *not* a racist.

Jeremiah Wright is *not* a racist.

Trinity United Church of Hate is *not* a racist church.

And if Wright, Obama, and Trinity United Church of Hate aren't racists, it's obvious that nothing a black person or group says or does can earn them that title.

Why?

Because "racist" means white person. Plain and simple.

Is it starting to sink in yet?

CHAPTER 12

Cops Are Racist!

Generally speaking, black people aren't very fond of police officers. Oh, I'm aware that there are exceptions, but anyone who thinks that there aren't millions and millions of black people in America who are filled with a deep and abiding hatred of law enforcement officers, is kidding themselves. When was the last time you saw a black group holding a banquet or other ceremony to honor the brave men and women who put their lives on the line every day to keep us safe? When was the last time you saw a black person organizing a fundraising drive to benefit the family of an officer killed in the line of duty? The last time? Most of us have never seen such a thing.

On the contrary, black groups are constantly attacking the police, all over the country, as a bunch of racists who get their kicks rounding up and brutalizing innocent blacks for no reason whatsoever. Any time a black thug gets shot, the local "civil rights" groups and phony reverends are all over the TV denouncing the officers who did what they had to do. On the extremely rare occasions when it turns out that the person who got shot truly didn't deserve it, but was the victim of mistaken identity or bad judgment under pressure, we hear about it for decades. Most black people seem to believe that the reason blacks go to prison at rates seven or eight times higher than whites is because they're framed by racist white cops in cahoots with a racist white judicial system. Anyone who thinks I'm exaggerating simply doesn't know what's really going on out there.

And, as you might have noticed, Barack Hussein Obama is black, so it should come as no surprise that he hates cops, too. At least the white ones, anyway. Of course, he didn't mention this before he was elected president. It came as a shock to his liberal white supporters, who thought Obama was a white man who just happens to have brown skin. And he's never actually come out and said he hates the cops; that wouldn't go over too well. It's best if he plays it cool, just like he did with William Ayers and Jeremiah Wright, and doesn't come right out and say the truth. That might alarm those evil honkies out in flyover country. But he made it quite clear in July of 2009.

Who can forget the weeks of "post-racialism" that ensued in the wake of the arrest of one of Obama's black pals, Henry Louis Gates, the Harvard professor who's also a radical left-winger who also just happens to hate white people? (Wright, Ayers, Gates...for a post-racial moderate, Obama sure does have some strange friends!) And if you think saying that Gates hates white people is too strong, then do a little research on him. Here's a little hint: you don't get appointed as a black professor at Harvard University by talking about how wonderful white folks are and how much you love them.

And if you're a white police officer, you don't arrest a black Harvard professor for disorderly conduct. James Crowley learned that the hard way. You get up every day and go to work trying to protect the lives and properties of the citizens of your town, and what thanks do you get? The President of the United

States denounces you on national television, that's what. There Officer Crowley was, trying to protect the home of Henry Louis Gates from a reported burglary attempt, and for his efforts he's screamed at and called a racist by Gates, and Barack Hussein Obama tells the whole country how stupid he thinks Crowley is.

You no doubt remember the story: Gates had just gotten back from a trip to China, and his door was jammed. So he and his companion began trying to force the door open. A concerned passerby saw what looked like a possible breaking-and-entering in progress and called the police. By the time Officer Crowley and the other police officers arrived on the scene, Gates and his friend had succeeded in getting into the house. Officer Crowley went to the open front door and informed Gates that he was there to check out a possible break in, and asked Gates to step outside. Now, if this happened to the average white person, we'd be happy and grateful that police were doing their job and had gotten there as fast as they did to try to protect our property. But Gates isn't a white man, and his response to the request to step outside was "Why? Because I'm a black man?" Gates' attitude and behavior went downhill from there, (at one point he yelled at Officer Crowley, "I'll speak to your mama outside!") and when he finally came outside and got more and more belligerent, he was arrested for disorderly conduct.

Well, the media had their "racist" story for the day, and boy was it a doozy. A black "intellectual" arrested in his own home by a racist cop simply because he was black! Before you could say hate crime hoax, the "racism" had hit the fan, and the story was all over the Internet and then the network and cable news shows. Of course, the mainstream media beat this dead horse for all it was worth. One angle was that "racial profiling" is alive and well, and that to those evil racist cops, a black Harvard professor looks just like a member of the Crips gang. The other angle, of course, was that even with a black president in office, nothing had really changed when it came to "racism," and there is still a long way to go before blacks are equal in the United States, and blah, blah, blah.

Poor Officer Crowley never knew what hit him. He was just trying to make sure that someone wasn't breaking into Gates' home — trying to protect a black man's property — when he finds himself being attacked all over the national media. Instead of being thanked and called a hero, he's attacked and called a racist. The left-wingers even started going after other Cambridge police officers. Liberal bloggers went ape when they discovered that one of James Crowley's fellow officers has a personalized license plate that spells out "WHY-TEE." Any normal person would look at that and think maybe the vehicle belonged to a disgusted ex-golfer, or that the driver's nickname was Whitey. Which was the case actually. The police officer who owns the vehicle had extremely blond hair as a kid, and the other kids called him Whitey. But that didn't matter to the liberals. All things white are evil, including the word itself, and they just knew that any white person who would drive around with a hateful word like that on their plates had to be a stone cold racist.[65]

On top of being demonized in the national media, Officer Crowley soon heard himself being denounced by the United States president. Barack Hussein Obama wasn't there at the scene of the arrest, but that didn't stop him from condemning James Crowley without knowing the facts of the case. He had all the facts he needed to form a decision. First, James Crowley is a white man. All white men are racist. Second, he's a police officer, and in the eyes of blacks, law enforcement is a racist institution in and of itself. Third, he had arrested a black man. What more proof did Obama need? None. When asked at a press conference about the Gates arrest here is what he said:

"Now, I've – I don't know, not having been there and not seeing all the facts, what role race played in that. But I think it's fair to say, number one, any of us would be pretty angry; number two, that the Cambridge police acted stupidly in arresting somebody when there was

---

[65] http://gawker.com/5322447/cambridge-cops-unfortunate-vanity-plate-why+tee

already proof that they were in their own home. And number three, what I think we know separate and apart from this incident is that there is a long history in this country of African-Americans and Latinos being stopped by law enforcement disproportionately. That's just a fact."[66]

Well, no, it's not a fact that black and brown people are stopped by law enforcement disproportionately. That's the big lie about racial profiling. It's true that blacks are stopped more often than white people, but it's not disproportionate at all. There is a very good reason blacks are stopped more often than whites — they commit crimes at far higher rates than white people. As I've discussed elsewhere, the black crime rate is about seven to eight times the white crime rate. If you're looking for criminals, you're naturally going to target the group with such an astronomically high crime rate. Any cop who doesn't simply isn't doing his job. In fact, as Ann Coulter has pointed out, given their astonishing crime rates compared to white people, blacks aren't pulled over nearly as often as they should be. The same principle holds true for Hispanics; their crime rates are lower than black crime rates, but still far higher than white crime rates.

Obama's remarks at the press conference didn't go over too well with white people across America; his approval numbers took a huge drop immediately afterward. Trying to repair the damage, Obama's handlers came up with the idea of "the Beer Summit," and invited Gates and Officer Crowley to have a beer with him at the White House. Gates accepted of course and, far too graciously, so did Crowley. This gave Obama a chance for a photo op to once again pretend to be the great healer who can bring whites and blacks together.

But the damage was done. Just as we did in February of 2009 when Eric Holder denounced us as "a nation of cowards" (meaning white people), white Americans got a glimpse into the

---

[66]http://en.wikipedia.org/wiki/Henry_Louis_Gates_arrest_controversy#Press_conference_and_briefing

true Barack Hussein Obama when he attacked Officer Crowley at the press conference. As if Holder's hateful remarks hadn't made it clear enough, Obama himself delivered the message loud and clear – he's not one of us, and his "post-racial" pose was nothing but a clever advertising scheme.

Obama is a black man first, and he shares the common black hatred of the police. He may not go around shouting "The cops and the Klan go hand in hand!" as black radicals did in the 1960s, but he clearly believes it. It's no wonder he and terrorist William Ayers are such good pals — Ayers is white, but his terrorist group the Weather Underground was known for killing white police officers, whom they called "pigs," in order to bring down the system of "white supremacy" in America.

CHAPTER 13

Van Jones: A Real Post-Racial Brotherhood Kinda Guy!

Say what you want about Barack Hussein Obama and the Democrats, but at least they're loyal to their voter base. Unlike the GOP, which would never do anything to advance the cause of their white base, Democrats take every opportunity to reward the non-whites who vote for them. They understand how politics works; if you want people to keep voting for you, you reward them when they support you. The GOP does the exact opposite. If the GOP leadership isn't denouncing its own base of supporters as a bunch of "racists," it's pandering to blacks and Hispanics who have never voted conservative, and never will. That's one of the reasons the Democrats are so successful. Their goal is to win elections, while the goal of the GOP is to avoid being called names by Democrats and the media.

So after George W. Bush won in 2000, he filled his administration with left leaning non-white people like Condoleezza Rice, Colin Powell, Alberto Gonzalez, Norman Mineta...you get the picture. He wasn't looking for the best person for the job; he was pandering to non-whites. As president, one of Bush's first acts was to order an end to "racial profiling," including at airports. What? You didn't hear about that? No, it's not something you're likely to hear from Rush, Sean, Glenn, or the other big "conservative" talk show hosts. They're not promoting conservatism; they're cheerleading for the GOP. And talking about the fact that Bush cracked down on "racial profiling" of Arabs at airports a few months before 9/11 isn't good for the Republican Party. But it's the truth.[67] Without Bush's crackdown, the World Trade towers might still be standing. And ten days after Arab terrorists attacked America, what did the Bush administration do?

On September 21, 2001, Mineta sent a letter to all U.S. airlines forbidding them from practicing racial profiling, or subjecting Middle Eastern or Muslim passengers to a heightened degree of pre-flight scrutiny. He stated that it was illegal for the airlines to discriminate against passengers based on their race, color, national or ethnic origin or religion. Subsequently, administrative enforcement actions were brought against three different airlines based on alleged contraventions of these rules, resulting in multi-million dollar settlements.[68]

Over three thousand Americans were slaughtered by Arab terrorists using jets as weapons. Ten days later Bush's priority was to not hurt the feelings of Arabs at airports. *That's* how Republican politicians thank their supporters. And don't even get me started on No Child Left Behind, which should have been called Destroying Good Public Schools in the Name of Equality. Or, even better, No White Kids Out In Front. The mortgage crisis which nearly brought down the entire economy before Bush left office? It was a direct result of Bush pressuring banks to lower lending standards so more non-whites could qualify for home ownership. [69, 70]

That's how the Republican Party thanks its supporters, by

[67]http://vdare.com/sailer/100110_diversity.htm
[68]http://en.wikipedia.org/wiki/Norman_Mineta#cite_ref-Commission_Hearing_3-1
[69]http://www.vdare.com/Sailer/080928_rove.htm
[70]http://blog.vdare.com/archives/2008/12/21/new-york-times-catching-up-to-steve-sailer/

pandering to the people who hate everything they stand for and will never vote for them in a million years. With unbelievably disastrous consequences. Both 9/11 and the mortgage crisis are partly the result of the Bush administration throwing common sense, public safety, and the entire economy to the wolves in order to be seen as non-racist.

But the Democrats? When they take the White House, do they fill their cabinet with conservative white Republicans? Do they start proposing policies that are good for you and your family, and defend them as good for conservative white people?

Uh, no. They reward the people who voted for them, not the ones who voted against them.

And Barack Hussein Obama, Mr. Post-Racial himself, is no exception. Except for the foolish whites who believed his lies about being post-racial; he has absolutely no problem stiffing them. Because they're white. Which means they're racists, and racists don't deserve anything, even if they're gullible enough to believe Obama's lies and vote for him.

Remember Van Jones? You may not; he was so radical and filled with hatred for white people that he didn't last very long. Moderate whites were shocked that Obama would appoint a man like Jones as his "Green Jobs Czar," but that simply shows they haven't been paying attention. Why should we be surprised that a man who would pal around with white-hating terrorist William Ayers, attend Trinity United Church of Hate for nearly twenty years, and name his book after Jeremiah "God damn America!!!" Wright, would have a problem with a radical black Marxist who hates white people? What exactly is shocking about that? The only surprise in the whole matter is that Obama didn't stick with him after the furor erupted.

In case you've forgotten, let me refresh your memory. Van Jones was an "environmental advocate" and "civil rights activist" chosen by Obama as Special Advisor for Green Jobs, Enterprise and Innovation at the White House Council on Environmental Quality (CEQ), or Green Jobs Czar as most people called it. He is an attorney who attended Yale Law School (almost certainly on a full affirmative action scholarship) and co-authored a book in 2008 called *The Green Collar Economy*. That's about all the media told us about Van Jones, if they mentioned him at all. But as his title of "civil rights activist" clearly signaled, there's a lot more to Jones than what the media was telling us. *A lot more.*

Like the fact that he took time out from his Yale Law School studies to riot in San Francisco after a Los Angeles jury refused to railroad four police officers who restrained a dangerous felon after he got violent. Yes, one of Van Jones' proudest accomplishments is being a part of the 1992 Rodney King riots, even if he missed the big show in LA, and could only take part in a smaller riot in San Francisco. Shortly after the riot, he wrote an essay bragging about his participation. Not long after the essay appeared, San Francisco police arrested him for his part in the riot.

Charges were dismissed, though, due to a politically correct district attorney who no doubt didn't want even more riots. Not only did Van Jones not suffer any consequences for rioting, he actually made money — the city gave him a settlement for arresting him after he boasted about rioting! Must be terrible to be an "oppressed minority" in America...

Jones is so proud of his participation in the Rodney King riot that in 2007 he republished his 15-year-old essay about it on Huffington Post. Here's a little sample of his essay:

We chanted our "no justice, no peace," blamed Reagan, blamed Bush, trashed downtown, and went home (or to jail). Still oppressed. Still clueless as to what to do about it.

Let's be clear: the riots were understandable, unavoidable, even necessary — but they were not laudable.[71]

Yes, the riots were understandable, unavoidable, and necessary in Van Jones' eyes. Something had to be done about

---

[71]http://www.huffingtonpost.com/van-jones/15-years-ago-rodney-king-_b_48361.html

Reagan and Bush, and all those evil racist honkies who keep voting Republican, so blacks had no choice but to riot, rampage and murder. Not only is Van Jones proud of taking part in the Rodney King riots, he also says that the experience profoundly changed him for the better:

I met all these young radical people of color — I mean really radical, communists and anarchists. And it was, like, 'This is what I need to be a part of.'...I spent the next ten years of my life working with a lot of those people I met in jail, trying to be a revolutionary.... I was a rowdy nationalist on April 28th, and then the verdicts came down on April 29th. By August, I was a communist.[72]

That was just the beginning! Here's what Wikipedia says hapened next:

"When he graduated from law school, Jones gave up plans to take a job in Washington, D.C., and moved to San Francisco instead. He got involved with Standing Together to Organize a Revolutionary Movement (STORM), a group explicitly committed to revolutionary Marxist politics whose points of unity were revolutionary democracy, revolutionary feminism, revolutionary internationalism, the central role of the working class, urban Marxism, and Third World Communism. While associated with STORM, Jones actively began protesting police brutality."[73]

You can see why Obama thought so highly of him. It's no surprise that a self-proclaimed communist would wind up as a big wheel in the environmental movement. Environmentalism is just one of the rackets radical Marxists shifted their focus

---

[72]http://www.conservapedia./Van_Jones
[73]http://en.wikipedia.org/wiki/Van_Jones

to when it became clear in the late 1950s that America wasn't quite ready for out and out communism; we would have to be moved toward it gradually. So the radical Marxists moved into environmentalism, education, religion, and whole host of other fields, including the big one, "civil rights." The goal is still "the redistribution of all wealth," as Jones explains here.

Right after Rosa Parks refused to give up her seat, if the civil rights leaders had jumped out and said, "OK now we want reparations for slavery, we want redistribution of all the wealth, and we want to legalize mixed marriages.'" If we'd come out with a maximum program the very next day, they'd been laughed at. Instead they came out with a very minimum. "We just want to integrate these buses."

But, inside that minimum demand was a very radical kernel that eventually meant that from 1964 to 1968 complete revolution was on the table for this country. And, I think that this green movement has to pursue those same steps and stages. Right now we say we want to move from suicidal gray capitalism to something eco-capitalism where at least we're not fast-tracking the destruction of the whole planet. Will that be enough? No, it won't be enough.

We want to go beyond the systems of exploitation and oppression altogether. But, that's a process and I think that's what's great about the movement that is beginning to emerge is that the crisis is so severe in terms of joblessness, violence and now ecological threats that people are willing to be both pragmatic and visionary. So the green economy will start off as a small subset and we are going to push it and push it and push it until it becomes the engine for transforming the whole society.[74]

And Jones, like any good communist/environmental advocate/civil rights activist (talk about a jack-of-all-trades), makes it clear he hates white people. We're the ones ruining the environment. It doesn't stop there, of course. Guess where us white racists are doing the most damage to the environment? If you guessed "in black neighborhoods," give yourself a pat on the back:

The environmental justice community that said, 'Hey, wait a minute, you know, you're regulating, but you're not regulating equally.' And the white polluters and the white environmentalists are essentially steering poison into the people-of-color communities, because they don't have a racial justice frame.[75]

He also thinks prisons are nothing but updated slave plantations, where innocent black people are locked up and forced to work for The Man by racist cops and a racist judicial system. In a June 2008 speech to the National Conference for Media Reform, Jones blasted a proposed prison in Memphis that he compared to a "huge slave ship on dry land."

"You don't have to call somebody the N-word if you can call them a felon," Jones said in the speech, which can be seen on YouTube. "The fight against this new Jim Crow, this punishment industry, where for-profit prison companies are now being traded on the stock exchange...that struggle is being met as it was forty years ago."[76]

And, oh yeah, he's a huge fan of cop killers. He even tried to turn one into a recording star. Yes, you read that right. In between his communism and his "environmental advocacy" and his "civil rights activism," Van Jones founded a record company, and produced a CD starring Mumia Abu-Jabal. Wait a minute; let me rephrase that...actually producing a record starring a

---

[74]http://www.foxnews.com/politics/2009/09/03/raw-data-van-jones-words/
[75]http://www.foxnews.com/politics/2009/09/03/raw-data-van-jones-words/
[76]http://www.foxnews.com/politics/2009/09/04/radicalization-obamas-green-czar/

convicted cop killer was part and parcel of Jones' "civil rights activism."

That's right; his "civil rights" group, the Ella Baker Center, produced a handful of CDs between 2002 and 2006. One of them, which appears to have been made around 2002, "starred" convicted murderer Mumia Abu-Jamal, who presumably recorded his portions of the album in prison.[77]

Yes, that's the man that "post-racial" Barack Hussein Obama wanted as a top member of his administration. After all this stuff started coming out, Van Jones eventually resigned, and in order to calm things down, the Obama White House said that they had somehow failed to properly vet Jones before appointing him. Yeah, right. Glenn Beck and a few bloggers can dig up this stuff on Jones but the White House missed it? I don't think so. Obama chose Van Jones because he knows exactly what he stands for, and he agrees with him. Before the uproar, Obama's right hand "soul sista" Valerie Jarrett even bragged about how "they" had been watching Jones for years and loved what he was all about:

Jarrett: You guys know Van Jones?

[Applause. Moderator injects: "This is his house apparently."]

Jarrett: Oooh. Van Jones, all right! So, Van Jones. We were so delighted to be able to recruit him into the White House. We were watching him, uh, really, he's not that old, for as long as he's been active out in Oakland. And all the creative ideas he has. And so now, we have captured that. And we have all that energy in the White House.[78]

There you go, white folks. Welcome to Barack Obama's "post-racial" America.

[77]http://www.powerlineblog.com/archives/2009/09/024444.php
[78]http://michellemalkin.com/2009/09/03/van-jones-valerie-jarrett-barack-obama-do-it-yourself -vetting/

CHAPTER 14

Some Things That Are Racist (And Some That Aren't)!

Writing this book was difficult because of the sheer volume of the subject matter. There is simply way too much of it; I could write thousands of pages about this stuff and it still wouldn't be enough. The hard part was deciding what to put in and what to leave out. Adding to the problem was that every day, as I was writing, I would learn about several new outrages, and I'd want to write about them, too. Eventually it became clear that I was just going to have to put my blinders on and ignore a lot of things, no matter how worthy of discussion, or I would never finish the book.

Then, once I'd settled on a fairly final list of topics, I had to decide how much each one deserved. Some topics, like John McCain virtually conceding the 2008 election so he wouldn't be called racist, obviously needed more words to flesh out. Likewise with Van Jones, Jeremiah Wright, and other topics. Others, though, while just as serious, didn't justify a few thousand words, but still had to be mentioned. So I decided to write some short snippets on these subjects, for your further edification and enjoyment.

Here's the first chapter full of snippets. Some of them are merely outrageous; others will make your blood boil. But all of them are just more evidence that "racist" means white person, and "racism" means anything a white person does.

THE AMERICAN FLAG IS RACIST!

Well, duh. The United States was founded by a bunch of white people, and it is still majority-white (although *that* won't last much longer) so, of course, the flag is racist. Besides, look how liberals and blacks treat the Confederate flag. It's a symbol of racism, oppression, and hate, and it should never be displayed in public. Doing so is tantamount to a hate crime. It doesn't matter that the Confederate flag is an important part of the heritage of millions of Americans, whose ancestors fought in the Civil War. No, anyone who says they're proud of their ancestors, or who would dare own or display a Confederate flag is an evil, wicked racist. Why? Because that flag flew over slavery. It's not just liberals and blacks who condemn the Confederate flag these days, more and more "conservatives" do it, too. Like John McCain for one, and many, many others.

I guess it never occurred to these geniuses that if the Confederate flag is hateful and racist because it flew over slavery for four years, then the Stars & Stripes must be extremely hateful and racist since it flew over slavery for nearly a hundred years. Liberals and conservatives alike will say that's different, because the Confederacy was established in support of slavery. So what? So was the United States. Slavery was written into the constitution! Many of our founding fathers, like Thomas Jefferson and George Washington, the Father of our Country, bought and sold slaves. If all traces of the Confederate flag have to go because of its association with slavery, it's only a matter of time until we have to abolish the Stars & Stripes and replace it with a new, "inclusive and diverse" flag that "represents all Americans," etc.[79]

That day is getting closer all the time. In 2009, there were two incidents where the American flag was banned — *in the United States of America* — for being "offensive" to non-white immigrants. To honor our veterans, Debbie McLucas put up a 3' x 5' flag in her office at Kindred Hospital in Mansfield, Texas, where she worked as a supervisor. Her husband and both her sons are military vets, and at the time, her daughter was serving in Iraq as a combat medic.

One day she arrived at work and was shocked to discover that the flag had been removed because it was "offensive" and there had been "multiple complaints" from people about it. One of the complainers was an African immigrant who works at the hospital.[80] After the uproar made national news, the hospital changed their story, saying that it was only taken down because it was too big, and they let Debbie McLucas put it back up.

In October of 2009, it happened again, this time in Albany, Oregon. Jim Clausen was flying an American flag on the back of his motorcycle to show support for his son who was about to return for another tour of duty in Iraq. But the manager of the apartment complex where he lived ordered him to remove the flag, threatening him with eviction if he refused. Other residents with American flags on their vehicles were given the same order — dump the Stars & Stripes or move. Several people told a local TV station the same story, saying "management told them the flags could be offensive because they live in a diverse community."[81] Once again, after an uproar, management backed down, and let residents continue to fly the American flag. For now. The fact that this could even happen in the "land of the free" should make it clear exactly where we're headed.

---

[79]http://www.vdare.com/fallon/confederate.htm
[80]http://www.foxnews.com/story/0,2933,522659,00.html
[81]http://www.katu.com/news/local/64059697.html

Refusing To Hire A White Man Is NOT Racist!

East St. Louis, Illinois is one of the filthiest, nastiest, most dangerous places in America. It's approximately 99 percent black, of course. I can't imagine why a white man would want to be police chief in that city, but apparently one or two had considered it. However, according to a lawsuit by two former city officials, the black mayor said the city "isn't ready to hire a white police chief."[82] For some reason, this wasn't considered newsworthy by the national media, although you can imagine their reaction if a white mayor flatly refused to consider any non-white candidates for a city position. That would be a major story, because it would be "racist," since it would be a white person discriminating by race.

High Gas Prices Are Racist!

Unfortunately, many conservative politicos and commentators have unwisely jumped on the bandwagon of calling their political opponents "racists," no matter how silly it makes them look. We saw this during the Harry Reid "uproar;" alleged conservatives denouncing a man for using the perfectly good word "Negro," as if he'd committed some sort of crime, for crying out loud. These conservatives obviously haven't quite figured out a couple of critical things when it comes to "racism" in this country, and don't understand why adopting this tactic never seems to work. They also seem oblivious to the fact that they usually betray important conservative principles when they try to "out liberal" the liberals. They need to read this book.

Kevin McCullough is a conservative radio talk show host who seems to think accusing people he disagrees with of "racism" is just the ticket to winning an argument. He's not as famous as Rush Limbaugh or Sean Hannity, but he's fairly well known,

---

[82]http://www.nationalpolicyinstitute.org/2009/10/30/suit-claims-east-st-louis-passed-up-white-police-chief-over-race/

and he's an online columnist for TownHall.com. Back when gas prices were going through the roof, McCullough thought he had hit on a great idea for bringing them down — blaming the high prices on racism:

"Spending $60, $70, even $90 for a fill-up at the gas station is fun right? When it comes to crippling racist and economically-debilitating energy policy, liberals have truly paralyzed America."[83]

Dude's a genius, I'm tellin' ya! So why is current energy policy racist? Because it encourages farmers to use corn for the production of ethanol. Okay. So what's racist about that? That corn could be going to feed African children, that's what is racist about it. Now there is no denying that there are big problems with our current energy policies. And using corn for ethanol is really very inefficient. But what in the world have African children got to do with anything? Since when do conservatives believe it's America's job to feed Africa? McCullough loves to criticize liberals for ignoring the constitution, but I'd love to see him point out where the federal government is authorized to feed the people of other nations. I can think of a lot of words to describe someone who cooks up crazy theories about how corn grown in Iowa somehow harms the welfare of Africans, and thinks this should be a factor in deciding on the best energy policies for America, but conservative isn't one of them.

WHITE FLIGHT IS RACIST! AND WHITES MOVING OUT OF BLACK NEIGHBORHOODS IS RACIST, TOO!

This one's a real doozy! During the 1960s and 70s, as "fair housing" laws proliferated, millions of black people began moving into white neighborhoods, along with a wave of crime, fatherless homes, low morals and the entire tangle of ghetto pathologies with them. It didn't take long for white folks to

---

[83]http://townhall.com/columnists/KevinMcCullough/2008/05/25/like_your_$5_gas

realize that in real life, racial integration was nothing like it was in all those public service TV ads, and they began moving out. This was called white flight. You may have heard something about it! In fact, we've been hearing about how evil it was pretty much non-stop for over forty years now. Even contemporary conservatives denounce it, and all right-thinking people agree that it was wicked and racist for white people to move when large numbers of blacks moved into their neighborhoods.

But now white people are moving into black neighborhoods, and it turns out that's racist, too! If you're bored one of these days, do an Internet search for "gentrification racism" or "gentrification racist." You'll find lots of interesting reading, condemning white people for doing the exact opposite of what we've been condemned for over the last half a century.

Out in Portland, Oregon, city officials decided that something had to be done about whites moving into black neighborhoods, so they organized an abomination called the Restorative Listening Project to lecture honkies on how racist they are for doing such a thing, and what they need to "understand" about how they're "harming" their new black neighbors by living next to them.

> *The goal of the project, which is sponsored by the city's Office of Neighborhood Involvement, is to have white people better understand the effect gentrification can have on the city's longtime black and other-minority neighborhoods by having minority residents tell what it is like to be on the receiving end. Once armed with a broader perspective, said Judith Mowry, the project's leader, whites should "make the commitment that the harm stops with us."*[84]

It got so bad that a nationally known radical left-wing homosexual spoke out against the hypocrisy. Here's what Dan Savage wrote in his *Stranger* blog:

---

[84]http://www.nytimes.com/2008/05/29/us/29portland.html?_r=1&hp

> *You know what? White people in the 60s and 70s that didn't want to live in racially mixed neighborhoods fled urban areas for the suburbs. It was called "white flight" and guilty white liberals everywhere agreed that white people sucked. Now white people are willing to live in racially mixed neighborhoods and it's called gentrification and guilty white liberals everywhere agree that white people suck.*
>
> *Sorry, guilty white liberals, but white people can't suck for fleeing racially mixed neighborhoods back then and then suck for moving into racially mixed neighborhoods now.*[85]

Actually, Dan, I think the whole point of "diversity" and "equality" is pretty much that white people suck, no matter what they do. They're white people, so whatever they do is "racist," by definition. It's hard to miss that point after reading this. White people are so racist that we're damned if we do, and damned if we don't. If we do A, we're racist, and if we do the exact opposite of A, we're racist.

It seems very odd, until you understand that "racist" simply means white person. Then it all makes sense.

---

[85]http://slog.thestranger.com/2008/05/theyre_doing_something_about_gentrificat

CHAPTER 15

More Things That Are Racist

GLOBAL WARMING IS RACIST!

Kids say the darndest things! Well, except when compared to black politicians. In another chapter I've written about the two idiot black politicians in Dallas – one of them a "judge" – who had no idea what the term "black hole" means, and took it as a racial slur. Then, rather than admit their ignorance of something any white 8th grader knows, they kept insisting that it's a "racist" term.

In 2008, a black congressman declared that global warming affects blacks more than it does whites. "Climate change is no longer just an environmental issue. It's now an issue of race, according to global warming activists and policy makers. It is critical our community be an integral and active part of the debate because African-Americans are disproportionately impacted by the effects of climate change economically, socially and through our health and well-being, House Majority Whip James Clyburn, D-S.C., said July 29."[86]

Is it just me, or does anyone else think that these politicians have a hole in their ozone layers?

LAW AND ORDER IS RACIST!

Unless you're a political junkie, you may not be aware of the latest development in the liberals' quest to demonize anything and everything conservative white people do, say or think. No worries, though; that's my job. I stay on top of this stuff, because I have a popular blog and radio show dealing with these topics. So what's the newest development? It's called "dog-whistle racism," and this one's a real beaut!

You know how dog whistles work, right? You blow on it, and humans don't hear anything because the frequency it emits is above our hearing range, but dogs can hear it just fine. Well, now the liberals are claiming that politicians (white ones, naturally) are using certain words and phrases this same way in order to appeal to us racist whites without everyone else catching one.

This is nothing new, of course. Until recently, liberals and blacks called this "speaking in code" or "coded racism," and went on about it constantly. I guess that was starting to sound old hat, and they needed a new phrase to capture the attention of white people who live in constant mortal fear of being perceived as racists, which is most of us. Plus, they can recycle their old articles about "coded racism," and get them republished by just changing a few words. There is always a big market in the mainstream media for articles denouncing white people as racists!

So what are these "dog whistle" words and phrases

---

politicians use, and what are their real meanings? Well, "law and order" is one of the most commonly cited ones. When a white candidate talks about the importance of "law and order," or promises to "get tough on crime," that's not what he or she really means. What is really being said is "I hate them damn Negroes as much as you do, and if you elect me I'll do my damndest to round up and imprison as many as I can, even if they've committed no crimes."

You can probably guess the other big one. Yep, it's "illegal immigration." When white folks running for office promise to do something about illegal immigration, what they're really saying is "I'm a racist who regards Mexicans as sub-humans who ought to be lined up and shot on sight, and if you vote for me, you can count on it happening!"

And we've all heard about "Joe Six Pack" in every election. It is now a racist dog-whistle term. Which is funny, because it's a term that politicians rarely use themselves; it has usually been media types doing election analyses or predictions that have talked about the "Joe Six Pack" vote. But in 2008, Hillary used the term, and even though she's a radical left-wing liberal who normally would never be accused of racism by other liberals, she was running against a black man, so pretty much everything she said was dog-whistle racism, including Joe Six Pack.[87]

And if you really want to see just how sick and twisted this whole "dog-whistle racism" thing is, just consider the phrase "soccer moms" for a second. We've all heard that phrase for years, and again, it was usually the talking heads on TV, not politicians themselves, who used it, to describe middle class suburban mothers, whose vote is critical for any politician. Of course, since the vast majority of middle class suburban moms whose kids play soccer are white women, the phrase "soccer moms" was soon denounced as "coded racism" by liberals and

---

[87]http://www.thepoliticalcesspool.org/jamesedwards/2008/10/24/joe-six-pack-is-racist-code/

blacks. Here's a snippet from a Huffington Post article from 2007:

> *In other words, when push comes to shove, the Democrats are just as likely to throw the gay folks and African-Americans and other communities they've courted overboard to appeal to presumably racist soccer moms and homophobic NASCAR dads...*[88]

But then, suddenly, and completely out of the blue, we were informed in 2008 that "soccer moms" was no longer "racist code," but was in fact the exact opposite — it now meant tolerant, open minded women of all creeds and colors. That's pretty weird. How does a term go from being an example of despicable race-baiting to being practically on a par with "rainbow coalition" seemingly overnight? It's very simple. Two words — Sarah Palin. When John McCain picked Sarah Palin, liberals went nuts. How dare McCain pick an attractive, wholesome white woman to be his running mate? Naturally, everything Sarah Palin said was "racist," and when she started talking about being a "hockey mom," because her kids played hockey, she was clearly using dog-whistle racism to attract white voters.

This is insane, of course.

She called herself a hockey mom because her kids really do play hockey, and there really aren't that many kids in America who play hockey, so it was hardly "code" of any kind. But the lunatic liberals knew better. Maybe most white kids don't play hockey, but virtually no black kids do, so, obviously when Sarah Palin said she was a "hockey mom" what she was really saying was "I hate Negroes!" And, just like that, the former racist term "soccer moms" became a liberal, inclusive phrase! I'm NOT making this up:

> *Interesting and revealing that, since the announcement*

---

[88] http://www.huffingtonpost.com/sally-kohn/larry-craigs-pullout-stra_b_63517.html

of Sarah Palin as Vice Presidential pick last Friday, the term "hockey mom" has been relentlessly repeated by Palin and the party to describe her. "Hockey mom" is a coded dog-whistle term for "White" and an aggressive alternative to the ubiquitous "Soccer Mom," and it wasn't chosen by the Republicans and Palin by accident.

Even the term "soccer mom" is a term of derision, connoting an overbearing, meddling type-A mother hen shuttling her brood around in a ghastly minivan (SUV today) while caring for nothing but her precious spawn and their ordained success and safety.

And underlying all of this is the sense by Americans that soccer is a faintly swish kids' game popular in screwed-up Europe and played elsewhere in the world by people of color. Sure, David Beckham was supposed to be the White face of soccer to break it in America, but his spectacular flame-out in LA and his stunning inability to kick a soccer ball off a London bus to the correct part of a ball field in the handover of the Olympics to London just weeks ago, together with his faintly gay "metrosexuality," make him more a reinforcement of what Americans hate in soccer rather than an emissary.

The code is clear: a "hockey mom" is a White, American mom; a "soccer mom" is a multi-culti, emasculating mom pushing a laughable "sport" to keep her children unhealthily sheltered and safe.

Sarah Palin and the Republicans know this racist code will resonate, and they're pushing it for all its worth.[89]

Really, folks. I couldn't make this stuff up if I tried. For years, "soccer moms" was supposedly dog whistle racism. Then Sarah Palin comes along, points out that she's a "hockey mom," and suddenly "hockey mom" is the work of the devil, and "soccer

[89]http://www.dailykos.com/story/2008/9/5/115318/5669/29/586798

moms" is fine and dandy.

What more proof do you need that all this "racism" garbage is simply made up on the fly in order to use any pretext, no matter how ludicrous, to demonize white people?

The word "racist" simply means a white person, and "racism" is anything a white person says or does.

Period.

CHAPTER 16

Now That's Entertainment!
And It's NOT Racist!

Now, if you're read this far, you're fully informed on how America is just filled to the brim with the scourge of "racism" — white people voting Republican, white people opposing Obamacare, white people supporting the cops, white people having the gall to criticize a black president, etc. It might seem as if there's no end to "racism," and that anything and everything is "racist." But if that's what you're thinking, you'd best think again. There are lots of things that are *not* racist, and it's important to know the difference. Let's look at some things that *aren't* racist.

HATRED OF WHITE ATHLETES IS NOT RACIST!

Let's talk about baseball, America's national pastime. Did you know that at one time Major League Baseball (MLB) didn't allow blacks to play? Nah, I'm just messin' with ya! Of course you did! Everyone knows that. Not only do we learn about

Jackie Robinson every year in school, but we also hear about him constantly on TV specials and news reports. And as if that weren't enough, MLB never stops reminding us about it. Every year there are more and more tributes to Jackie Robinson during the Major League Baseball season. It's getting so out of hand that they should just change their name from Major League Baseball to the Jackie Robinson All Day Every Day Baseball League.

Every April 15 is now Jackie Robinson Day, and to help celebrate, every player, coach and umpire in every game on April 15 wears Jackie Robinson's #42 on his uniform. And just to prove that MLB has no concept of what running something into the ground means, Jackie Robinson Day is accompanied by "civil rights summits" and lots of special events for black kids, and just about every black person who's ever been on the radio or TV will be throwing out the first pitch or singing the national anthem at a game somewhere.[90] This is MLB's way of telling everyone, over and over and over and over, how progressive they are. "Look at us! Oh, my but aren't we tolerant! We actually allow black people to play!" It's pretty pathetic to be building your whole league image around something that happened nearly 70 years ago, but that's political correctness for you.

But what's really galling is that on top of this, the bigwigs of Major League Baseball (as well as many commentators in both news and sports) are always lamenting that there "aren't enough blacks" in baseball, and what a shameful tragedy this is, and how they've just got to do more to take jobs away from white players and give them to black players.[91] Which is very strange, when you think about it, because the percentage of black major leaguers is just a little less than the percentage of blacks in America's population (8.4% vs 13%).[92] That is, it's strange unless you realize that anything that's good for whites, like getting high paying jobs in baseball, is "racist," and anything that reduces the number of whites in any group is "pursuing Diversity," etc., etc.

---

[90]http://mlb.mlb.com/news/press_releases/press_release.
[91]http://thesop.org/story/sports/2007/04/06/the-outsourcing-of-major-league-baseball.php
[92]http://money.cnn.com/2007/04/13/commentary/sportsbiz/index.htm

Whites are actually underrepresented in professional baseball, being about 72% of the population but only about 60% of MLB players. But no one ever suggests that something needs to be done to remedy *that* situation; that would be "racist."

What's even more amazing is that while all these liberals and race hustlers are always always attacking Major League Baseball, the National Hockey League and NASCAR (with the help of the groveling execs in all three sports), they never say a word about how insanely out of whack the racial percentages are in the National Football League and the National Basketball Association. In the NFL, about 70% of the players are black. In the NBA the racial disparity is even worse, with blacks making up 80% of the league's players.

Blacks make up only about 13% of America's population, so these figures are simply astonishing. If liberals and race hustlers were honest, and really meant what they say about fairness, equality, inclusion and "racism," they'd be raising no end of hell about this, and demanding that something be done about discrimination against whites in football and basketball. They do no such thing, of course. In fact, the NBA is regularly praised for being a "model of Diversity"![93] Which ought to tell you something, white folks — "Diversity" doesn't include you. The average American thinks Diversity means a mix of all races and colors. It means no such thing. Diversity means non-whites, and "promoting Diversity" means replacing white people with black and brown people.

Not only are liberals and race hustlers not bothered by blacks being vastly overrepresented in the NBA and the NFL, they then turn around and use it as a basis for even more racial shakedowns! They tell us that because almost all the players are black, it naturally follows that the percentage of black coaches, general managers and owners should reflect these same percentages! What hypocrisy. In baseball, hockey and auto racing, the sports where whites come closest to reflecting their percentage of the population, these same frauds tell us there are too many whites, and that more blacks must be recruited, even in baseball, where blacks are only slightly underrepresented (and so are whites.) They certainly don't go around demanding that more white managers and GMs be hired because so many players are white. But in the NBA and the NFL, where blacks are wildly overrepresented, they don't demand that teams recruit white players; they insist that blacks be given even more jobs. Their claimed "principles" of Equality and fairness are all lies. All they care about is what's good for blacks, and bad for whites. If blacks are a minority, we need more of them. If blacks are a majority, we need more of them. Heads blacks win, tails whites lose.

When you think about it for just a few minutes, it becomes pretty clear where we're headed. In sports where whites are only slightly overrepresented, more blacks must be given jobs. In sports where the black percentages are five to six times their share of the population, more blacks must be given jobs. It's hard to avoid the conclusion that liberals and race hustlers won't be satisfied until zero white people are in professional sports. And if you point out this abominable double standard and complain about it, guess what that makes you? Yep, you got it — you're a "racist."

Using The Media To Demonize And Ridicule White People Is NOT Racist!

Ah, Hollywood! Where do I start? Tinseltown is run by liberals who hate ordinary white people, and boy does it show. Never in the history of the world has there been anything with the power of today's media. They decide what we think about, how we think about it, what we talk about, how we're allowed to talk about it, etc. Oh sure, their power is a tiny bit less than it was a few years ago thanks to the Internet, but we're kidding ourselves if we think Hollywood and the rest of the media don't set the agenda for most people in this country. If, as scientists tell us, our brains are magnificent computers, then TV, movies and music are the software to our brains' hardware.

It's impossible to overestimate the power of the media to condition Americans to think "the right way" about things. The Hollywood elites are aware of their power, and how useful it is; they don't turn it on full blast, for fear of waking us up. If they just repeatedly hit us over the head with blatant propaganda, most people would realize what was going on. So they're much more subtle about it. They know they have all the time in the world, so they gradually brainwash people over years and decades, not in one night. The pace is accelerating, lately, as they see how effective they've been and are trying to push the envelope. Just as the news media covering the Tea Parties and Obamacare protests can't hide their hatred of white people, neither can Hollywood. (Actually, in today's world of media conglomerates, the entertainment and news media are increasingly the same thing.)

If you doubt it, just consider Madison Avenue. It's run by the same type of people who run Hollywood, and if you want to know what they think of white people, just watch a few TV commercials. The hatred of white people that's displayed in TV ads is so blatant that it's hard to believe more of us haven't noticed it, but evidently few have. That's the power of gradual propaganda; things change so slowly that most people don't even notice. It's like the old story about the frog. If you drop a frog into a pot of boiling water, he'll immediately hop out. But drop that same frog into a pot of lukewarm water, and very gradually heat it, and he'll sit there until he boils to death.

That's exactly what's been happening to white people in the media for the past few decades, and it's been so subtle and gradual that we haven't even noticed what's happening. Well, it's time to wake up, because the water is starting to get really hot. If you doubt it, start watching TV ads with a critical eye. Most people don't; they've blinded themselves to the absolute contempt white people are subjected to in more and more TV commercials. If you think I'm just blowing smoke, then try a little experiment. The next time you're watching a ball game, or any other TV programming for an extended period, keep a little note pad with you, and take a few notes about the ads you see. I think you'll be amazed.

What you'll find is that whites in TV commercials, especially white men, are constantly held up as objects of ridicule and hatred. They're humiliated, made to look stupid, silly, spineless, helpless, obnoxious, contemptible, and in more and more cases, evil. To top it off, they're almost always paired with a non-white, usually a black person, who's the exact opposite — he or she is smart, quick witted, well dressed, good natured and has it all together. The non-white characters are often made to express exasperation, disgust or contempt at their white counterpart in the ads. So go ahead and do the experiment. Write down how many ads you see, how many characters are in them, how many of the doofus/bad guy characters are white, and how many of the smart guy/hero characters are black or Hispanic or Asian. I guarantee you — you will be shocked. If you've never paid any attention to TV ads before, prepare to have your mind blown.

This trend really kicked into high gear back in the 1990s. One of the worst offenders back then was America Online (AOL). They had a series of ads explaining the benefits of their service and the commercials were extremely brazen in their contempt for white people. In the series, and there must have been five or six different ads, one character would ask a really idiotic question, like "how do I buy stamps to send an e-mail?," or something equally ridiculous. Then another person would patiently explain to them, after rolling their eyes or something, that e-mail didn't require postage stamps. In each and every one of these ads, the doofus was a white man, and the person who explained things to them was a non-white. In some ads it was a Hispanic, in some it was an Asian, and in some it was a black person. But the moron was never anyone but a white man, and the helpful, smart person was always non-white.

Nowadays, though, it's not just AOL. Just about every major company takes this tack in their ads. ESPN does it constantly in their own ads for their networks, even though white male viewers are their bread and butter. That doesn't matter; white people are worthy of nothing but contempt in the eyes of the media and major corporations. There used to be an exception to this — investment and financial planning companies, and a few other companies selling high end products or services, never used to run ads expressing contempt for whites. Even that has changed, though. While watching the 2010 NCAA basketball championships I discovered that even these firms are jumping on the white-people-are-stupid-or-evil bandwagon in their ads.

One of the ones I saw was for the big financial firm ING. You can watch in on YouTube.[94] It showed a white man trimming his hedges in his suburban neighborhood. A well-dressed black man approached, and he was carrying a big piece of wood or plastic in the form of a number, something like $1,108,623. The white guy asked the black man what the number was. He replied that it was how much he needed to save for a comfortable retirement. The camera pans back, and we see sitting on the white guy's hedges the same sort of thing, except it just has the nonsensical term GAZILLION. The black man asks incredulously, as if he can't believe how stupid this white doofus is but doesn't want to be rude, "is that your number?" The idiot white man says "yeah, a gazillion, bazillion...it's just a guestimation." The black man asks him how he plans for that, and the moron replies "I blindly throw money at it and hope something good happens," and laughs. "So you really don't have a plan?," the black man asks, and the white doofus replies "I really don't," and then sheepishly goes back to trimming his hedges.

This may seem mild, and if it were the only example it would be no big deal. But it's not. Virtually every other commercial these days is a variation on the stupid/evil white guy paired with the smart/nice black person theme. Another one I saw was for a different financial company. I can't find it on the internet, but this one featured an evil white man trying to rip off a black man, who was thankfully too smart to fall for it. It showed two well-dressed middle aged men out on the golf course. One was

[94]http://www.youtube.com/watch?v=Zbl_hzSiK8M

black and one was white. The black man, as he lines up his putt, says "You want me to invest in imported ice?!" The white guy replies that with imported water being so popular, imported ice is bound to be the next big thing. The black man is having none of it, and asks why, if people want imported ice, they can't just freeze imported water. Really nice, huh? An evil white broker or financial planner trying to rip off a black man by talking him into a ridiculously absurd investment.

During the 2010 Super Bowl, Careerbuilder.com ran an ad that didn't even bother trying to hide their contempt for white people. The ad was making fun of "Casual Fridays" in offices, where people can dress down, instead of wearing the usual business attire. At the huge office in the ad, people had taken it to an extreme, and were walking around in nothing but briefs for men, and bras and panties for women. Now, you've seen enough ads to know that it's practically unheard of anymore to have any group of people bigger than three that is all white. You *never* see all-white groups of people in TV ads. It just isn't done. With one exception — when you want to humiliate or ridicule people, it's fine to make all of them white. Which is just what Careerbuilder.com did. They showed literally scores of people walking around in their underwear, and except for two fleeting figures way in the background, every single one of them was white. Naturally, none of them were attractive; they were pasty, out of shape, and even downright fat. You can also watch this commercial on YouTube.[95] Take a look at it and ask yourself when was the last time you saw that many people in a TV ad, and they were all white. The casting was no accident; the ad was deliberately designed to make white people objects of ridicule. If you think it was just accidental, then do another experiment. Go to YouTube and look up a bunch of commercials for home security companies, such as Brinks. There are lots of them, and most of them feature terrifying scenarios of people in their homes with a criminal trying to break in. I dare you to find one that shows a non-white criminal!

---

[95]http://www.youtube.com/watch?v=zMi3bd_ulKU

Remember Washington Mutual (WaMu), the mortgage company that went under because they were passing out mortgages to unqualified home buyers like they were candy? WaMu was notorious for its anti-white hatred. Go to YouTube and look up "Washington Mutual ad" or "Washington Mutual commercial" and see just how bad they were for yourself. Their running "gag" was that they weren't like old fashioned bankers, and to demonstrate it they had a group of about thirty "old fashioned bankers" they ridiculed and humiliated in their ads. WaMu contrasted them with their personable spokesman, "Bill." Naturally, every single one of the greedy, evil, senile, contemptible stupid bankers was white, and just as predictably, "Bill" was black. In one of the ads, "Bill" locked up all the old white men in some sort of pen, and then teased them by making them bob for champagne. Every one of their ads was like that; young, cool, affable and black "Bill" ridiculing and humiliating a bunch of callous, venal, greedy, old white men.

It gets even worse, believe it or not. In early 2009, black singer Rihanna went to Los Angeles police and filed a domestic violence complaint against her boyfriend, the black singer Chris Brown. She claimed he had put her in a headlock, bit her ear and finger, punched her in the face repeatedly, and threatened to kill her.[96] A few weeks later an organization called DoSomething. org created a public service ad around the incident. During the two minute video, while a narrator read from the actual police report, two actors re-enact the vicious assault. And the actors were white![97] That's right; a famous black man beats the living daylights out of his famous black girlfriend, but in the "re-enactment" white actors were used! It doesn't get much clearer than that, folks. The head of the outfit that made the ad, Nancy Lublin, said they used white actors to put the focus on domestic violence and not on Chris Brown and Rihanna. Yeah, right... No, they did it because you never show black people in a bad light in ads; only white people. Does anyone really believe that if had been Britney Spears who'd gotten beaten up by Justin

[96]http://www.cnn.com/2010/SHOWBIZ/Music/02/04/chris.rihanna.year.later/index.html
[97]http://www.mtv.com/news/articles/1607405/20090320/rihanna.jhtml

Timberlake that they would've used black actors? Of course not; that would be "racist."

As much as Madison Avenue hates white people, Hollywood itself is even worse. They constantly portray the people of middle America and the South as ignorant, violent, inbred rednecks with a raging hatred of non-whites. They've been doing it for half a century now, and they've been so effective that many white people themselves have come to believe that most (or at least tens of millions of) other whites are filled with hate for blacks and Hispanics and are just itching to kill a few. That's why movies and TV shows packed with liberal lies about "racism" are usually quite popular — they allow brainwashed whites to congratulate themselves on their moral superiority to all those millions and millions of "racist" white people who are supposedly out there.

Think of all the movies, TV show episodes and mini-series you've seen during your lifetime about the "civil rights" movement, Martin Luther King, Jr., Jim Crow, slavery, etc. If you're an average American, you've seen hundreds, and they're still cranking them out, in order to keep stoking white guilt. Most of them are filled with lies, and the writers and directors commonly toss in incidents of gratuitous and horrific violence just for fun. They know that not one white person in a hundred will actually go consult a history book to find out what really happened, so they can portray the white characters in these productions as the worst kinds of monsters, and they'll never be called on it, and whites will think even more badly of their own people. It's a win-win!

The double standard doesn't stop there, either. Back in the 1960s and early 1970s, Hollywood and the rest of the media glorified Lenny Bruce and George Carlin as heroes, because they were repeatedly being arrested for saying "bad words" in their act. In fact, Carlin's most famous routine was "The Seven Words You Can't Say On Television." To hear Hollywood tell it, Bruce and Carlin were fighting for freedom of speech and standing up against censorship, which is always wrong. That was a lie, though. They didn't love Bruce and Carlin for fighting censorship; they loved them because their obscenity offended white Christian Americans. Nowadays, of course, you can hear several of Carlin's famous seven words on TV every night of the week, and you can hear all of them if you have cable or satellite. But censorship hasn't gone away; it's just been replaced by a different kind, and Hollywood is the biggest enforcer of the censorship code.

Of course, the current censorship code only applies to white people, and it's in place to make sure that white people don't say anything non-whites or liberals don't approve of. Offending white Christians is terrific, and can make a two bit comedian like Carlin or Bruce a hero in the entertainment industry, but a white person saying anything a black or brown person disagrees with is strictly taboo. Just ask Michael Richards, of "*Seinfeld*" fame. I'm sure everyone remembers the uproar a few years ago after he got mad at some black guys in the audience who were talking during his comedy act, and in a lame attempt to be "outrageous" and "provocative," called one of them "the N-word."

It was a stupid thing to do, but hardly newsworthy. Nevertheless, it became one of the top stories on every national news broadcast and thousands of websites. It stayed in the news for months, and all sorts of Hollywood types came crawling out of the woodwork to condemn Richards, and talk about what a vile, disgusting person he was. Never mind that this was the very same crowd that had just offered Dave Chappelle $50 million to produce more episodes of his popular TV show, on which about every third word uttered was "the N word," and which portrayed blacks in the worst stereotypes possible — crackheads, thieves, welfare mamas and ghetto trash whose only care in the world was getting more bling bling. When a black guy does that, it's great, and Hollywood offers him $50 million; when Michael Richards used the word one time in a fit of anger, he became toast, and basically hasn't worked since. By now, though, you understand why — Richards is white, so he's a racist. Dave Chappelle is black, so no matter how racially inflammatory his show is, it's not racist.

Actor Jamie Foxx famously said after the incident that if he ever ran into Richards, he would physically attack him,[98] and was given the hero's treatment by the media. Never mind that Jamie Foxx has a radio show where he regularly uses the word. In fact, he recently called Howard Stern's black sidekick Robin Quivers "Howard's house n*gger."[99] Oh, and a couple years after threatening to assault a white man for using "the N word," Foxx called 16-year-old Miley Cyrus "a little white b*tch," and urged her to become a lesbian, make a sex tape, and "catch chlamydia on a bike seat."[100] But I'll bet you never heard about that, did you? Of course not; there was no uproar in the media over what Foxx said about a white girl. That's OK, see, because Jamie Foxx is black! He can say horrible things about a white girl, and that's NOT racist. He can't be a racist, because "racist" means white person.

(If you still don't get it, ask Don Imus to explain it to you...)

The double standard in Hollywood is just for starters. What's even worse is the active poisoning of people's minds by the entertainment industry.

Ever heard of a movie called *"River's Edge"*? It came out in 1986, and it was about a group of kids in California. One of them murdered a girl, and not only bragged to his friends about it, but took a bunch of them out to see the body over the course of a few days, but nobody bothered to call the police. It's considered an "important" movie, and there's no denying that it had a profound affect on many of the young people who saw it. The movie is based on a true story, which took place in Milpitas, California in 1981. When I say it's based on a true story, I should probably use quotation marks. That's because in the movie, the killer and the jaded, callous kids were white. In real life, the killer and his friends were black. Of course, I'm sure the director would tell you he only used white actors to portray such callousness and brutality

[98]http://www.hollywood.com/news/Foxx_Threatens_Racist_Richards/3588998
[99]http://www.jewishjournal.com/seriousstern/item/howard_stern_v_jamie_foxx_20100405/
[100]http://www.eonline.com/uberblog/b118545_jamie_foxx_slams_miley_cyrus_make_sex.html

because he didn't want the real killer to be "a distraction," just like DoSomething.org and their PSA about Chris Brown beating up Rihanna, wink wink.

This kind of thing would be bad enough if it only took place in an occasional movie or two. Unfortunately, that's not the case. In fact, many of the most popular TV shows do this very same thing week after week, year after year. Everyone in America is familiar with the series *Law & Order* (*L&O*) and its various spin offs. For twenty years *L&O* has been one of the most popular shows on TV, and its spin offs have been very successful as well. These shows often feature plots that are "ripped from the headlines," in other words, they're based on true stories. Except for one thing — many, if not most, of the real life murders that become script material are committed by black or brown people, but on the show they're turned into white people. As Steve Sailer puts it:

> *"Indeed, it's possible that more murders are committed annually by fictional Great White Defendants on the L&O shows than by real whites in all of New York City. From 2003 through 2005, there have only been an average of 27 homicides per year in Manhattan south of Harlem, where most L&O episodes are set, or about six percent of all murders in New York City.*

> *"You might think that the news media might have noticed that Law & Order has become a very silly show. But that would require the press mentioning that blacks and Hispanics commit more violent crimes than whites do, which, as [series creator Dick Wolfe] Wolfe points out, would be in the worst possible taste."*[101]

Independent journalist Nicholas Stix wrote about this phenomenon of *L&O* portraying black and brown murderers as white several years ago. His article is a must-read.[102] Here

---

[101]http://www.vdare.com/sailer/060430_unequal_justice.htm

[102]http://nicholasstixuncensored.blogspot.com/2009/12/nbcs-law-order-anti-white-propaganda-in.html

are a couple of "highlights" from it: In an episode that aired in February 2001, a real-life murder by several black kids who ordered Chinese food and then killed the delivery man, is the "basis" of the plot, but on the TV show, the murderers are a bunch of white kids from good homes. In May 2003, there was an episode based on the D.C. snipers, John Muhammad and Lee Malvo, who were, as I'm sure you remember, black Muslims. In the TV show the D.C. Sniper magically became a white man.

Not all *L&O* plots are based on true stories. As Stix makes clear, the writers and producers manage to come up with all sorts of gruesome and heinous murder scenarios on their own, and in these outrageous scripts, the homicidal maniacs are almost always white. Of course, *L&O* is hardly alone in that. Crime shows are very popular, and every week they bring us a new crop of evil white people creating mayhem and killing innocent people. Is it any wonder that millions of people in this country have no idea who's responsible for so much of the violent crime in America?

And it just keep getting better and better, folks. The hot new trend is to portray white people as terrorists victimizing innocent Muslims and committing "honor killings"![103] I kid you not — this past December, just in time for Christmas, the hit show *NCIS* featured a story line where a young Marine is found murdered. We find out he had just converted to Islam. Then we learn several more things. His father was a Christian preacher, actually a Marine chaplain, and he had been paying his son's military buddies to harass him, hoping to make him "de-convert." Then it turns out that the dead soldier's wife, also a white Christian, had been cheating on him. And guess who killed the poor Muslim? His own brother — it was an honor killing. The dead solider had disgraced the family name by converting to Islam and had to pay. Wow; just like real life, huh? Dad, a Christian preacher, paying his buddies to harass his own son. His Christian wife was an adulterer. And his Christian brother murdered him. Gosh, I wonder where all the anti-white

---

[103]http://newsbusters.org/blogs/mike-sargent/2009/12/16/ncis-series-goes-way-law-order

and anti-Christian prejudice in this country comes from?

That same week, a spin off show, *NCIS: Los Angeles*, had a similar story line. Four wounded Marines come back from Iraq. One is murdered by an exploding cell phone; the other three are apparently nearly killed, too. Suspicion quickly turns to one of the surviving three Marines, who's a Muslim, and is acting strangely. But in the end, it turns out alright. We find out the Muslim wasn't the killer, it was one of the other two Marines, who was a devout Christian. You know how those white Christians are! Merry Christmas from Hollywood, you evil racist white people!

Hollywood is poisoning the minds of tens of millions of people every week with this kind of garbage. In real life, murderers are overwhelmingly black or brown; on TV, they're almost all white. That's no accident. Hollywood doesn't want people to know the ugly racial realities about crime, so they make white people out to be the people who are committing almost all of the violent crimes in America. Then these same people have the gall to turn around and call the Tea Parties "racist," because there are only a few blacks at their rallies!

Chapter 17

Still More Things That Are Racist (And Some That Aren't)!

Ham Sandwiches Are Racist!

Ham sandwiches are not only racist, they're a hate crime! No, I am not making this up. Back in the late 1990s, Bill Clinton decided that America needed more African Muslims than we were already importing every year, and authorized the resettlement of thousands of backward Muslims from Somalia in America as "refugees." (Yes, this was Clinton's doing, but please don't fall for the "Democrats bad/GOP good" trap that Limbaugh and Hannity and Palin are trying to sell you — Bush did absolutely nothing to curb Muslim immigration to the US after 9/11, and it was his crackdown on "racial profiling" in February 2001 that helped bring about 9/11.)

Well, for some reason, thousands of these Somalis began settling in the small town of Lewiston, Maine. Many of them wound up on welfare — in 2008, unemployment among

Lewiston Somalis was 51 percent.[104] However, they're all black, so they're entitled to privileged treatment from white people. Plus, they're Muslims, and ever since 9/11 this nation has been groveling to Muslims pretty much non-stop, from the White House on down.

So a few years ago, when someone set a bag containing a ham sandwich on a table at a Lewis school where a bunch of black Somalis were eating their lunches, all hell broke loose. What should've been seen as a childish prank at worst, and in a different light could be seen as boys being boys and trying to make friends by being silly, or quite possibly was a kid just setting a lunch bag on a lunch table, became *the hate crime of the week* in not just the local Maine media, but all over the national news, both on TV and the Internet.

The Lewiston Police department actually began an investigation of a ham sandwich as a hate crime! A group called the Center for Prevention of Hate Violence got involved, helping the local schools come up with an appropriate "response" to this dastardly hate crime. The poor kid got suspended, too. Imagine that! A school child being suspended…for setting a lunch bag on a lunch table! In America, the so-called Land of the Free and Home of the Brave![105]

Banning White Kids From College Prep Classes Is NOT Racist!

The ACT is a rigorous college entrance exam, taken by tens of thousands of high school juniors every year. It's scored on a scale of 0-36. A high score on the exam can not only determine if a student gets accepted by a competitive university, but can also mean thousands of dollars in scholarship money to help defray the ever-increasing cost of attending college. Because a good score is so important, students and parents all over America pay hundreds and hundreds of dollars for weekend

[104]http://en.wikipedia.org/wiki/Lewiston,_Maine#Somali_and_Bantu_migration
[105]http://www.americanthinker.com/2007/05/the_ham_sandwich_hate_crime.html

ACT cram sessions held by various companies. Prepping kids for the ACT is a lucrative industry because students and their parents understand just how crucial it is to do well on the test, because a high score can make all the difference in the world for the kid's future.

Well, one innovative teacher at a Chicago area public school got to thinking — if a prep course consisting of only a weekend or two helps kids do better on the ACT, what would happen if the school offered a year long weekly class to help kids do better on the test? She went to the administration with her idea, and they approved it.

So, every week, all year long, the class at Waubonsie Valley High School prepped for the ACT test, boning up on the various subject areas, and taking lots of practice tests.

Now the results are in, and they're pretty amazing. Black kids who took her class wound up raising their scores on the ACT about 5-6 points over their scores on a practice exam they took at the beginning of the year. On a scale of 36, that's huge. It's pretty remarkable proof that a yearlong, comprehensive and intensive approach to raising student's academic achievement can work wonders. Any student who sits for the ACT after taking this yearlong prep class is going to have an enormous advantage over kids who didn't.

Wow James, that's pretty impressive. How'd the white kids do?

White kids? This class is for blacks only.

Those racist white kids can go to hell.

Math teacher Natalie Johnson raised more than a few eyebrows last fall when she suggested Waubonsie Valley High School offer an all-black ACT prep class.

But one year later, her efforts to close the achievement gap between white and minority students at the Aurora school seem to be working.[106]

---

[106]http://www.dailyherald.com/story/?id=214692&src=5

That's how you close the achievement gap — by screwing over the white kids, and giving the black kids tons of extra attention.

BANNING WHITE KIDS FROM COLLEGE SCHOLARSHIPS IS NOT RACIST!

Bill Gates is famous for being one of the richest men in the world. He made his billions by founding Microsoft, and after he retired he wanted to "give something back." So he set aside a billion dollars out of his massive fortune to fund full, four year college scholarships for deserving young people. Pretty nice of him, huh? Well, Bill Gates has a funny definition of "deserving." To him, it means "not white." That's right; Gates Millennium Scholarship are off limits to white kids. Gates makes no bones about it.

"Students are eligible to be considered for a GMS scholarship if they are: African American, American Indian/ Alaska Native, Asian and Pacific Islander American, or Hispanic American."[107]

Does that take gall or what? Bill Gates is a white man, and the vast majority of people who made him a multi-billionaire by buying his products are white, and he turns around and kicks us in the teeth by telling us that our children aren't good enough for his college scholarships!

It would be nice if some billionaire would set up a scholarship fund just for white kids.

But that will never happen. Why? Because that would be "racist"!

TACOS ARE HATE CRIMES, TOO!

If racist ham sandwiches aren't crazy enough, things are even worse in Cincinnati, Ohio. At a magnet school there, the Academy of World Languages, the racism and hate have

---

[107]http://blog.vdare.com/archives/2010/02/02/bill-gates-scholarships-exclude-white-kids/

gone far beyond ham sandwiches. Yes, as horrible as it is to contemplate—and I sure hope you're sitting down as you're reading this— there's no denying the ugly hate and racism in Cincinnati: a Hindu kid ate a taco![108]

No, I'm not joking. A Hindu kid eating a taco not only became a national news story, it also became the subject of a federal investigation by the U.S. Department of Justice! Why? Because the taco had beef in it. The school says the kid ate the taco of his own accord, which sounds pretty believable. But the Hindu father claimed in a letter to the Department of Justice (DOJ) that the school forced the beef taco on the kid, in an intentional act of religious bigotry (Hindus don't eat beef).[109]

Clearly, this is none of the government's business, especially the federal government's. But because of race, a molehill had to become a mountain, and a federal case was made of a taco. Sure, the non-white Hindu dad is accusing the school of religious bigotry, but every one of us knows that if this were a white Mormon who had filed a "civil rights" complaint because his kid had drunk a forbidden cola or tea at school, the DOJ would have laughed in his face, and probably told him to quit filing frivolous complaints or face charges himself. But when the kid is non-white, a taco is both a hate crime and a federal case.

DENIGRATING WHITE ATHLETICISM IS NOT RACIST!

Uh-oh! There I go again. Using a racially tinged word like "denigrate" which comes from the Latin word, *nigrare*, "to blacken."

Let's consider football. At the upper echelon of play, the NCAA Division 1 and NFL, whites are rarely, if ever, allowed to participate in positions like cornerback or running back. Other positions, such as safety and wide receiver, seem to be a rapidly closing door for white players.

---

[108]http://www.thepoliticalcesspool.org/jamesedwards/2009/06/15/justice-department-investigating-a-taco/
[109]http://www.littleindia.com/news/128/ARTICLE/5162/2009-07-05.html

One would think that such obvious racial underrepresentation would get media attention. If you did, you'd be confused and apparently not understand that white players can *never* be underrepresented.

A few years ago, Pete Prisco, CBS Sportsline.com Senior Writer had the courage to write about the mystery and scarcity as to why there was only a single starting NFL center that was black. Just so his article wouldn't be accused of overlooking the obvious, he states in a brief aside, "To think skin color plays an issue in any position anymore would be sad. The belief here is that the best players play, regardless of position. There are no white cornerbacks starting in the NFL, but that's for skill reasons. Nothing else. So an issue isn't made about it."[110]

There you have it! White players don't have the SKILL to play cornerback, but the reason there aren't more black centers must be due to...you guessed it, discrimination and latent RACISM among NFL player personnel that apparently have the lingering racist belief that "the quarterback position and the center position were considered to be the cerebral positions and blacks, African-Americans, weren't considered intelligent enough to handle the workload."

In fact, one possible explanation for the scarcity of black centers is that the black centers that come into the NFL are so athletic that coaches move them to a position that requires more athleticism, such as guard or tackle!

However, the desire for more black centers pales (uh-oh another racist term) in comparison to the desire for more black quarterbacks (the marquee spotlight position on a football team).

Completely ignoring the zero white starting running backs or cornerbacks in the NFL, one of the biggest concerns in the media is the apparent lack of black quarterbacks, since out of the 36 most active quarterbacks in the NFL in 2009, only seven of them are black or 19.4%, which is a higher percentage of black quarterbacks than their percentage (13%) of the entire US population.

There are zero white starting running backs or cornerbacks,

---

but the bigger news is not that there aren't any black quarterbacks, it's just that there aren't an even more overwhelming percentage of them!

If you ask any liberal football fan if they would like for there to be more successful black quarterbacks in the NFL, they would be quick to establish their credentials with an affirmative answer. Yet when Rush Limbaugh made a comment that "the media has been very desirous that a black quarterback do well," he was forced to *resign* from his job on the ESPN NFL pre-game show! How dare he point out the obvious!

In fact, his infraction was so extreme by liberal standards that years later when he tried to buy a minority ownership in an NFL team, there was a tremendous outcry that he be denied the opportunity. So much for "the only color that matters is the green of his dollars." Good thing he didn't sing a song by pop artists J-Lo or Fergie on his radio show! Their vulgar lyrics, which include the N-word, might have gotten Rush banned from even attending an NFL game!

However, J-Lo and Fergie just happen to be part owners of the Miami Dolphins, but since they aren't as white as Rush, they apparently can say whatever they want.

How hypocritical! We're all supposed to want more diversity (don't forget that diversity only means more non-whites, not just more variety), yet when someone says that more diversity and minority success is being sought after (the thing we're all supposed to want), they get attacked for it. So we're supposed to want black success, but we're not supposed to *talk* about wanting black success. Seems clear as mud.

I admit it can get confusing, or at least to those that don't understand that if a white commentator is talking about race it's bad and racist. When a non-white talks about race, no matter how outrageous it is, that's just fine, such as when black commentator Michael Irvin said that for Tony Romo (the Dallas Cowboys quarterback) to be so athletic, his genealogy had to include "some brothers....Great, great, great, great Grandma pulled one of them studs up outta the barn."[111]

If you follow football commentators at all, you'll start to understand.

Great white player = student-of-the-game, cerebral player, always-know-where-the-ball-is-going-to-be, high motor, great work ethic, faster-than-he-looks, sneaky or deceptive speed, surprisingly quick, lots of drive and determination (basically, they're overachievers trying to make up for their lack of athleticism).

Great non-white players = athlete.

White athleticism has become a liberal oxymoron.

Even video game developers are starting to understand. An ESPN article from a couple of years ago mentioned that there was an NCAA video game, in which if you created a fictional black player with certain attributes, it labeled the player as an "all-purpose back." If you kept every other attribute the same, and changed him to a white player, he became a "power back."[112]

In case you didn't understand the difference, all-purpose backs are considered more talented and athletic. Power backs are supposed to be plodding brutes that just plow through the line of scrimmage without any finesse.

To pick one example of the stereotypes that white players have to fight against, consider Toby Gerhart. In high school, Toby broke the California High School career rushing record by more than 1,000 yards! However, what did major collegiate programs like USC see in Gerhart – a fullback, designed to block for other "more athletic" running backs. They even tried to get him to switch to defense and play linebacker, another "white approved" position.[113]

Instead of getting to play for a perennial football powerhouse like USC, Gerhart went to Stanford where he was able to play tailback and get to actually carry the ball. He rewarded Stanford in his 2009 senior season by leading the nation in college football with 1,871 rushing yards and 28 touchdowns.

[111]http://blogcritics.org/sports/article/fire-michael-irvin/

[112]http://sports.espn.go.com/espn/page2/story?page=hill/080926

[113]http://cbs5.com/sports/Toby.Gerhart.racism.2.1650279.html

He paid USC back for ignoring him by rushing for 178 yards and three TDs in Stanford's 55-21 victory over USC in 2009.

He also managed to win the Doak Walker Award (given to the nation's best college running back) and come in second for the Heisman Trophy (given to the nation's best college football player).

Stats such as those generally lead to a high first-round draft pick, unless you happen to be a running back with the wrong skin color.

At the 2010 NFL combine, Gerhart brought up the question of "Why was [he] the only running back who had to run under 4.6 to not be classified as a fullback? Fifteen other guys ran in the 4.6s at the combine, and nothing was said about them [playing fullback]."

If you guessed that those fifteen other guys were non-white, you'd be right. A Yahoo! Sports article revealed the depths of bias that he faced:

"Race shouldn't be an issue, of course, but Gerhart can't help but believe that it has colored the opinions of at least some potential employers.

"One team I interviewed with asked me about being a white running back," Gerhart says. "They asked if it made me feel entitled, or like I felt I was a poster child for white running backs. I said, 'No, I'm just out there playing ball. I don't think about that.' I didn't really know what to say."

"One longtime NFL scout insisted that Gerhart's skin color will likely prevent the Pac-10's offensive player of the year from being drafted in Thursday's first round.

"He'll be a great second-round pickup for somebody, but I guarantee you if he was the exact same guy – but he was black – he'd go in the first round for sure."[114]

---

[114]http://sports.yahoo.com/nfl/news?slug=ms-gerhartstereotype042010

Imagine if you will that same scenario happening because a player was black. There would be riots in the streets and demands for reparations.

But it's okay when it happens to a white player, because that's NOT Racism!

COTTON BALLS ARE RACIST!

Better think twice before you remove that cotton ball from the aspirin jar, white man! And white ladies had best be sure they properly dispose of any cotton balls they use to remove makeup. Dropping cotton balls on the ground can now mean spending months or years in prison!

But only if you're white.

See, if you're black, or Mexican, or Hindu, or Chinese, and you drop some cotton balls on the ground, that's a misdemeanor. If you're caught, you'll pay a small fine at worst, and most of the time you'd probably just get a friendly warning or lecture from the authorities.

Of course, that's fine. Society has nothing to fear from cotton balls dropped by blacks, Mexicans, Hindus or Asians. That's because they're not evil racist white people, so the cotton balls are as harmless as they look when members of these groups drop them on the ground, and there's nothing to worry about except picking them up.

But when evil racist white people drop those cotton balls, they're magically transformed into atomic hate bombs, as shown by this story from February 2010:

> *"Two University of Missouri students have been arrested on suspicion of hate crimes after cotton balls were scattered outside the Black Culture Center.*

> *"Campus police arrested a 19-year-old freshman and a 21-year-old senior Tuesday night based on an anony-*

mous tip. The two men face possible charges of felony
tampering and have been suspended from school.[115]

The two young white men arrested were Zachary Tucker
and Sean Fitzgerald.[116] According to reports, they had engaged
in several pranks that night, like riding the statue of the school
mascot, and hoisting a pirate flag."[117]

It's just a shame that a little harmless fun turned into a
regular Kristallnacht. After the cotton balls were discovered in
front of the Black Culture Center, hundreds of black students
packed the place to talk about how unsafe they felt on campus
now.

That's right. They felt unsafe. Because of cotton balls. No,
I'm not kidding.

And, by the way, don't bother asking if the University of
Missouri has a White Culture Center. Of course they don't; that
would be racist. And asking why it's OK for blacks to have one,
but not whites, is racist, too. So just zip it, pal!

INTIMIDATING WHITE VOTERS IS NOT RACIST!

Boy, some days it seems like anything and everything
is racist. Tacos are racist, ham sandwiches are hate crimes,
cotton balls are racist hate crimes, etc. Is there no limit to what
constitutes racism any more? That's the question on the minds
of a lot of people these days. Well, good news, folks! It seems
that if two members of the New Black Panthers hate group are
standing outside a polling place on election day, dressed in
paramilitary uniforms, and brandishing weapons, using racial
slurs against whites, and telling white voters that Obama had
better win because whitey has had his way long enough...that's
NOT racism!

---

[115]http://www.kansascity.com/2010/03/03/1786577/two-missouri-students-arrested.html
[116]http://beforeitsnews.com/news/22570/Two_students_arrested_for_cotton_ball_hate_crime.
   html
[117]http://www.wnd.com/index.php?fa=PAGE.view&pageId=127592

You may remember this incident — it occurred on Election Day 2008 in Philadelphia, PA. FOX News reported it, and several videos of the incident made it onto the Internet, where they amassed hundreds of thousands of views overnight. It was shocking to see such blatant, race-based voter intimidation in the 21st century. But there it was. And even though the perpetrators were black, and the victims were white, the conduct was so outrageous that the Justice Department opened a case against three members of the New Black Panther Party for intimidating white voters on the basis of race. Then, in May 2009, with Eric Holder, the guy who hates racism at the helm, the Department of Justice announced they were dropping the charges.

Well, not all charges were dropped. The Black Panther who brandished the weapon was actually punished. His punishment?

He's not allowed to brandish a weapon within 100 feet of a polling place. Well, not until the 2012 elections are over, anyway. Then he can start doing it again.[118] And, no, once again, I'm not making this up.

People were outraged but that's because, as I've said over and over in this book, they haven't been paying attention. If they had been, they wouldn't have been surprised at all. Only white people can be racist. And everything white people do is racist, whether it's serving tacos, setting a lunch bag on a lunch table, or dropping cotton balls on the ground. Blacks and other non-whites, by definition, can't be racist, and so nothing they do can be considered racism. Case closed.

Are you starting to get it yet?

---

[118]http://www.amren.com/mtnews/archives/2009/07/gop_holder_batt.php

Chapter 18

Conclusion:
Where Do We Go From Here?

Well, here we are, folks. We've come to the end of the book. It didn't take that long, did it? (This final chapter's going to be short and sweet, too.) And, hopefully, if you've read this far it's because I've convinced you — "racist" is just a code word for white people, and that as long as we keep recoiling in horror at the sound of the word, we're never going to be able to roll back the juggernaut of liberalism and big government.

I'm kind of sad about reaching the end of writing this book. That's for a couple reasons. First, this book shouldn't even be necessary. It's been getting increasingly obvious, for years now, that "racist" doesn't mean someone who hates members of other races and wants to harm them (which is the definition most white people think of when they hear the word). Instead, it has become nothing but a racial slur directed at white people in order to shame us into voting, believing or behaving a certain way. In other words, liberals and non-whites use the word to "keep us in our place." And boy, have we learned our place! We react to words like "racist" and "racism" the same way Superman reacts to Kryptonite or a vampire reacts to a cross. Constantly crying "racism" is the most brilliant idea liberals have ever had. They can't sell their plans on their merits, because there aren't any, but they can sure intimidate us into shutting up and going along with the program with that magic six-letter word. Yet hardly anyone has noticed what they are doing to us. A few have, but we still have a long, long way to go.

That's because far, far too many of the good folks on the conservative end of the political spectrum have allowed the liberals to use "the R-word" to silence us. And I'm not using hyperbole, or exaggerating at all. We've been so intimidated by the word that we're starting to lose our freedom to speak out about issues. As I write this, Ann Coulter is in the national news, and all over conservative political websites and blogs. Why? Because, while on a speaking tour of Canada, one of her scheduled appearances was canceled as a result of the hysteria over "racism" and "hate" that liberals have manufactured out of thin air and applied to any and every conservative. She was supposed to speak at the University of Ottawa, but leftists were slinging words like "racist" and "hatemonger" at Coulter all over the media in the weeks before her appearance.

On top of this, a university administrator warned Coulter not to transgress Canada's notorious "anti-hate" laws, stirring up even more prejudice against the conservative commentator. The liberals were pulling out all the stops, and they got what they wanted — so many protesters showed up threatening to disrupt the meeting that it had to be called off due to fears of violence.

This is outrageous. What good is free speech in principle if thugs and hooligans can prevent a conservative from actually exercising this precious God-given right because they disagree with it, simply by labeling it "racism" or "hate?"

A lot of folks reading this will agree that what happened to Ann Coulter is appalling, and it's truly unfortunate that free speech appears to be dying in Canada, but it's really no cause for alarm here in America. After all, we have the First Amendment to the Constitution, so that could never happen here. So what goes on in Canada is really neither here nor there, and there's no need to be concerned about the right to free speech in the United States.

Well, my friend, if that's what you think, you need to think again. Because not only can such a trampling of free speech occur right here in the USA, it already has. Not just once, but twice.

I should know, because the first time it happened I was at the center of the controversy.[119] Back in 2008, I helped organize a conference for the conservative European-American Unity and Rights Organization (EURO) near the Memphis, Tennessee area, which I was also scheduled to co-host. EURO is a peaceful, law abiding group formed in order to do just what the name implies — to foster unity among American of European descent, and speak up for their rights. Blacks, Hispanics, Asians, Jews and other racial groups have created hundreds of similar groups for the benefit of their people, such as the NAACP, the League of United Latin American Citizens (LULAC), La Raza and on and on.

Powerful outfits like these are countless, and exist for every non-white group in America, but except for a few tiny groups like EURO, there is not a single organization in America speaking up for the interests of white people. As a conservative talk show host based out of the Memphis area, I wanted to do my part to help this fledgling organization, and I spent weeks making the arrangements for the conference, lining up speakers, booking the venue, getting the word out via my blog and radio show, etc. It was hard work, but very rewarding, and putting the 2008 EURO conference together will always be one of the things I'll be most proud of when looking back on my life.

Unfortunately, I'll also have to remember that time as one of the saddest periods of my life. That's because, at the last minute, even after speakers and guests had begun arriving in town for the conference, the hotel where it was to be held canceled the conference. Why? Because local law enforcement officials had declared a "state of emergency" because of all the threats the hotel was getting. People were calling the manager

---

[119]http://www.thepoliticalcesspool.org/jamesedwards/2008/11/10/euphoric-conference-held-against-all-odds/

of the hotel at his home, threatening to kill him and his family if he allowed "racists" to hold a conference at the hotel. It seems that white people aren't allowed under any circumstances to get together to talk about their interests or rights, or even to think of ourselves as a group at all, even though non-whites have hundreds of groups representing their ethnic interests.

Now, you can just imagine what the response would be if a hotel or convention center manager was getting phone calls at his home threatening to kill him and his family if he allowed the NAACP to hold a conference. Number one, it would be all over the national media. Secondly, local, state and federal law enforcement would kick into high gear, doing everything they possibly could to protect the safety of the conference speakers and attendees. And rightly so. But white people? If people phone in death threats against a white group, somehow we're the bad guys! And I'm certain you never heard about the EURO conference being canceled due to terrorist death threats. Not even the conservative blogs, websites or radio talked about it. Why? Because liberals had declared us "racists," and so conservatives didn't want to speak up for our rights of free speech and assembly.

In early 2010, the very same thing happened again, this time right in the heart of the nation's capital, when the 9th American Renaissance conference was canceled due to death threats against hotel management and employees.[120] *American Renaissance* (AmRen), founded by Jared Taylor, is a monthly magazine that challenges the mainstream dogmas about Diversity and Pluralism. It's a thoughtful and intelligent magazine, and every two years it holds a conference to discuss these topics. It's been doing this since 1994, and C-SPAN even broadcast one of their conferences a few years back. Speakers over the years have included prominent academics, journalists, and politicians. Jared Taylor is a graduate of Yale University, and a well-known author himself. But, because *American Renaissance* doesn't parrot all the PC platitudes about race, Jared and the magazine

---

[120]http://www.vdare.com/hart/100216_anarcho_tyranny.htm

are regularly condemned as "racists" in the press.

There have been a few scruffy looking protesters at past AmRen conferences, but the meetings have always gone off without a hitch. Not in 2010, though. As soon as this year's AmRen meeting was announced, leftists began contacting the hotel and, just as they did in Memphis, issuing death threats to workers and managers where the conference was to be held. The hotel caved in, and canceled the meeting in spite of a signed contract, just like in Memphis. AmRen found another hotel, but the same terrorists began issuing their threats anew, and it, too, canceled. So did another one. Finally, at the last minute, a fourth hotel agreed to host the conference. Jared had been upfront with them about the circumstances, and hotel management assured him there would be no problem, as they were committed to standing up for free speech in America. Unbelievably, they too backed down and canceled the meeting at the last minute, after many people had already gotten on planes to attend. Once again, terrorists were able to deprive people of their rights to free speech and assembly, because they were guilty of the sin of being white.

Again, this happened not just in the United States of America, "land of the free and home of the brave," whose First Amendment to the Constitution used to be the envy of the world — it happened in Washington, D.C., the nation's capital. And not a damned thing was done about it. For all the talk about the war on terrorism, you'd think the FBI and the Department of Homeland Security would be making it one of their highest priorities to find out who was responsible for phoning in death threats to American citizens in order to shut down free speech. But you would be wrong. They couldn't care less, because white people are "racists," and shouldn't be allowed to get together as a group.

I'm willing to bet that this is the first you've heard about this episode. Just as with the terrorism that shut down the Memphis EURO conference, the national media was silent. Jared Taylor sent out a press release, but the media had more important things to worry about than a bunch of "racists" whining about their "rights." Racists don't have any rights, so AmRen deserved what it got. But it wasn't just the liberal media that took this attitude. The conservative media was shockingly silent about this outrage. Rush Limbaugh, Sean Hannity, Glenn Beck...not a peep from any of them, or any coverage on conservative websites or blogs. They're silent when Americans are deprived of their free speech right here in the nation's capital, but they go ballistic when Ann Coulter is silenced in Canada. The right-wing media literally spent weeks discussing that episode. Do you see anything wrong with this picture?

Look, folks, we'd better wake up before it's too late. Conservatives have become so afraid of the word "racist" that they won't even speak up about what happened to EURO and AmRen. Instead, they pretend they didn't see it, and give consent by their silence. Apparently we're all hoping that the liberals and non-whites will notice that we didn't utter a peep about these things, like good little boys and girls, and maybe in return they'll stop calling us racists, because we're not like those "real racists" at EURO and AmRen.

Well, besides being cowardly and dishonorable, that approach won't work. As I think I've clearly demonstrated in this book, to liberals, "racist" means conservative white person. Sure, today they're just denying the rights of EURO and AmRen, but it won't stop there. One thing you can count on with liberals is that they'll just keep moving the goal posts. If you doubt that, try this little experiment. Go to AmRen's website at www.amren.com. Spend some time reading it then go to a library or Internet archive and peruse some issues of National Review from the 1960s and 1970s. You'll find that Jared Taylor and AmRen simply talk about race the very same way that William F. Buckley and *National Review* used to discuss race.[121] If Buckley were a young writer today, conservative talk show hosts would be denouncing him as a "racist," and no bookstore would sell *National Review*. What

---

[121]http://www.amren.com/ar/2000/09/#cover

was the mainstream of conservative thought just a few decades ago, is now complete anathema. Liberals know exactly what they're doing; it's time we figured it out, too, and stopped letting them do it to us.

This groveling and kowtowing to liberals has got to stop. We can no longer let them set the rules that we're going to play by if we ever hope to achieve any kind of conservative renewal in America. If we don't draw a line in the sand, right now, they'll soon be doing to all of us what they did to AmRen and EURO. But as long as we keep making it clear that we're terrified of being called racists, they'll keep doing it. Why shouldn't they? It's been the most effective tool they ever dreamed up.

So what do we do? Simple. First, understand one thing — when a liberal says "racist," they mean a conservative white person. It's just their way of terrifying us into doing one of two things: either shutting up, or wasting all our time trying to prove we're not racist, instead of working on accomplishing our political goals. Look how much time has been wasted just these past few years by conservatives who spent millions of man-hours denying that they were racist for voting against Obama, or denying that they were racist for opposing his stimulus plan, or denying that they were racist for opposing socialized medicine, etc., etc. When we do that, we're just playing the liberals' game. When we're always on the ropes, we can't put up much of a fight.

So from now on, quit playing their game. Instead of constantly denying that you're a racist, just ignore it. Laugh in their faces, because now you understand that to them "racist" just means a conservative white person. Don't waste your time trying to "prove" you're not a racist. It's a hopeless task, and it's pointless. If you're a conservative white person, you're a "racist" to a liberal, and you always will be, as long as you remain true to your conservative convictions. And, for crying out loud, let's quit playing the pathetic token game. Appointing unqualified affirmative action types to positions of leadership in conservatism is a recipe for disaster, as we've seen with Michael

Steele. He's the head of the Republican Party for one reason, and one reason only — because he's black, and man, has that worked out well...

So just stop falling into this trap. No more tokens, no more arguing, no more trying to "prove" we're not racists. They're going to call us that anyway, so what's the point? You're just wasting your time and energy. Like the famous Tea Party sign said: "It doesn't matter what this sign says, you'll call it racist!" Whoever came up with that brilliant slogan has obviously understood what I've spent this book spelling out in detail: "racist" is simply a slur liberals use against conservative white people. That sign's attitude is the attitude we all need.

Don't deny.

Don't argue.

Don't try to prove you're not a "racist."

Just laugh in their face. Then counter-attack. Point out how whites in this country just want a level playing field, and that it is the minority groups who want racist preferences. Tell them they're obsessed with race instead of what's best for our country. Expose their bigotry and anti-white racism as they seek to portray all conservative white Americans as "racists." Never let them get to you, never feel guilty for who you are or where you came from.

When enough of us start doing that, we can start taking this nation back!

ABOUT THE AUTHOR

James Edwards
Host

James Edwards is the creator and primary host of "The Political Cesspool Radio Program," an award-winning broadcast that has gained national attention for conducting interviews featuring columnist Pat Buchanan, author Jerome Corsi, rocker Ted Nugent, and countless other headliners and newsmakers.

The success of TPC has made James a media magnet, earning him numerous appearances on CNN, while the show itself has been the subject of articles in the *Los Angeles Times,* the *London Times, Newsweek* and other major print publications.

James has received a certificate of recognition from the Memphis City Council for "Outstanding Contributions to the Community," and has been named Honorary City Councilman.

He continues to host his syndicated talk show while making time to speak at various political functions and conventions throughout the year. He has previously served as a contributor to the *American Free Press* newspaper and, as a private pilot, holds membership at a local flight club.

He resides in Memphis with his wife.

8219567R0

Made in the USA
Charleston, SC
19 May 2011